T0285805

BE
THE
ONE

BE
THE
ONE

THE UNIVERSAL ROADMAP TO CREATE, DESIGN, AND LIVE AN UNFORGETTABLE LIFE

BY JUSTIN PRINCE
WITH CLAY MANLEY

Foreword by *New York Times* bestselling author,
John C. Maxwell

Published by Maxwell Leadership Publishing, an imprint of Forefront Books.
Distributed by Simon & Schuster.

Library of Congress Control Number: 2023910826

Print ISBN: 979-8-88710-028-9
E-book ISBN: 979-8-88710-029-6

Cover Design by Bruce Gore, Gore Studio, Inc.
Interior Design by PerfecType, Nashville, TN

This book is dedicated to you, the person who is striving, working, planning, praying, and doing everything they can to "be the one" for their family, to live a live worth remembering, and to make a difference in this world. You and I are kindred souls, bound by our shared desire to make a positive impact on our world . . . and *the* world. This book is my way of fulfilling a promise to you, a promise that if I ever achieved *my* dreams and goals, I would help as many others as humanly possible to achieve *their* dreams and goals. I hope the lessons in these pages inspire and empower you to do just that.

CONTENTS

FOREWORD

by John C. Maxwell

My friend, the great Zig Ziglar, wrote the foreword for my first *New York Times* bestselling book, *The 21 Irrefutable Laws of Leadership*. Today, I'm honored to write this foreword for my friend Justin Prince's first published book, *Be the One*.

I have been a student of personal growth, leadership, and success for more than fifty years, and I've been a teacher, leader, and mentor to millions for many of those years. When I first met Justin Prince, like me, he was an eager student. Since then, I've had the privilege of watching him grow into a great teacher, leader, and mentor as well.

Today, Justin is a teacher who shares many of my same leadership principles and values. A mentor who values people and adds value to people. And a leader who knows the way, goes the way, and shows the way. That's why I've trusted him as a partner, cocreator, and collaborator on several of my key projects and initiatives—from traveling abroad with me and my team to transform entire countries and inspire global leaders to guiding the next generation of students and leaders through my virtual courses and live events.

But what makes Justin great is not only his incredible business accomplishments and accolades. It is his *personal* accomplishments and accolades that stand out to me. That's why I consider him a rare, complete, 360-degree person.

Justin Prince isn't just a great business leader. He is a great parent. A great spouse. A great friend. A great mentor. And now, a great author.

In fact, Justin once said of me, "John is a true leader. He practices what he preaches. In fact, John is not only as good as you would hope he would be; he is much, much better."

I would say the same of him.

Like all "great" people, you must develop yourself to be successful. Through his personal transformation, Justin has developed a roadmap for success that he has distilled into this book. A roadmap that, if followed closely, will guarantee you be all you can be. A complete, 360-degree person, like him.

Rather than a purely motivational book, this book is more like an instructional manual. In each chapter, you will find a new "step" to success revealed. Each step is illustrated with powerful examples, making it simple to understand and practical to apply. You will discover not just what to do to achieve success in every area of your life, but how to do it. Because the largest gap in the world is between knowing and doing.

I believe this book will finally bridge that gap for you, the reader.

In the following pages, you will be introduced to the concept of "being the one." And you will quickly see and understand why you already are "the one." Then when you take the steps Justin shares, you will "be the one." You will "be the one" to your clients. To your colleagues. To your friends. To your family. In your professional and your personal life. And by "being the one," your story will live on long after you're gone. In other words, this book will both maximize your life and cement your legacy by showing you how to "be the one."

In 1998, my friend Zig Ziglar welcomed readers like you to my world. Today, I'm honored to welcome you to my friend Justin Prince's world. Read on to "be the one."

INTRODUCTION

Who is "the One"?

It was a cool Memorial Day morning in southern Utah. My oldest son, Isaac, and I hopped in my car, and I pointed it east to Escalante, three hours away. The vehicle's headlights illuminated towering red rocks and empty pullouts overlooking canyons and vistas, which would later be packed with eager admirers at a more appropriate hour. As my son and I neared our destination, the rest of the world finally began to stir. We made a quick pit stop to the first florist shop to flicker open to collect a kaleidoscope of red, yellow, and orange flowers, which would mark this special occasion. Eventually, we rolled up to the aging, steel welcome sign hanging over the entrance gate, arriving just as the warm sun illuminated the flat, neon green landscape lined with cement-gray tombstones. The long rows of rectangular shapes extended until they met a brown backdrop of rocky hills and mountains.

The truth is, I had never met the man we had trekked to Escalante Cemetery to visit. Nor had Isaac. Yet, to my amazement, my teenage son spent several minutes kneeling beside his headstone.

I silently absorbed the tender moment, intentionally fading into the background just a few feet away. I knew not to interrupt, but I did wonder, *What was Isaac doing down there? Was he crying or praying . . . or what?* When he finally rose to his feet, I asked him.

"I was thanking George," Isaac replied, calmly and with conviction.

"For *what*?" I asked.

"For his hope, courage, and resilience."

And then he shared something I'll never forget: "I was thanking George for being 'the one.'"

George Prince, the man we were paying our respects to on that Memorial Day morning, is my fifth-generation grandfather, and Isaac's sixth-generation grandfather.

He passed away so long ago, it would be no surprise to anyone if George was a total stranger to me. Let alone to my son. At best, his would be a name we could barely remember. His story as unfamiliar as the oblong tombstones and headstones that surrounded his.

But more than one hundred years later, a full century after his passing, George's story is near and dear to me. It's near and dear to Isaac. And it's near and dear to my entire family. His life's journey is familiar to us.

Before I continue, I'd like you to pause. Take a minute to think about you and *your* family. Picture the loved ones in your life. Allow the details of their faces to fill your mind. Relive a precious moment or two. Page through the familiar chapters of their stories.

My friend, this book isn't about me and my family. It's about you and your family. More importantly, it's about guiding you to "be the one" for your family—in this one and only life you get.

Isaac and I have a shared understanding of "the one," which became clear as day as we placed that honorary flower arrangement on George's grave together. And that's why I'd like to share George's story with you now, to illustrate an example of someone being "the one," and to clarify our destination as we begin this journey together.

In 1841, decades before the very first automobile hit the streets or the first airplane took to the skies, George Prince led his family on a grueling eight-thousand-mile voyage across continents. To put that in perspective, eight thousand miles is the equivalent of traveling from Seattle to Miami *and* back—with hundreds of miles to spare.

Forget the cars and planes that make today's travel a breeze. Back then, the only means of getting from one place to another were slow-rolling wagons guided by unreliable horses, dilapidated boats with flimsy white sails forced to trust the unpredictable elements to lead them to their destination . . . or any destination, and perhaps the most dependable means of all, your own two feet.

At the time, thousands of English emigrants like George had been granted free passage to leave England and to colonize land elsewhere. For many, land meant opportunity. Opportunity the Princes couldn't pass up.

George and his family gathered the few possessions they had and embarked on what they thought would be the most prosperous adventure of their lives: a challenging and treacherous journey from England to what would eventually become South Africa. It was a journey driven by George's hope, courage, and resilience. And his vision of a better life. The travelers included George, his wife, Sarah (my fifth-generation grandmother), their eleven-month-old son, Francis (my fourth-generation grandfather), and George's brother, John (my fifth-generation uncle).

Soon after they arrived in Africa to claim their "promised land," after weeks—months—of dicey and exhausting travel via wagon, boat, and foot, the tired family found themselves under attack. Indigenous warriors had flocked to the area that was being colonized, with cowhide shields, bladed spears, and other weapons and firearms they'd collected en route—essentially turning the free land the Princes and others had been granted into a bloody battlefield. Imagine that. After an almost-impossible eight-thousand-mile journey, or fight, for a better life, the Princes were now forced to fight for their very lives.

The family had no clue these indigenous warriors had been ravaging European settlements for some time. But they quickly learned of the horrible damage they could do and the unthinkable pain they could inflict. During these deadly battles, now known as the Xhosa Wars, the warriors would target and capture young British boys.

Why boys?

To eliminate their opportunity to grow up . . . so that they could never become soldiers. After all, soldiers are trained to fight. And in this case, to fight back.

Francis was around five years old when the wars were at their worst, and the innocent young boy essentially walked around with a bullseye on his chest. And a potentially torturous bullseye at that.

It is difficult to describe this, and may be difficult for you to read, but according to the journals that commemorate George's journey, these warriors would trap immigrants—males like George, John, and Francis—rip all the clothing off their bodies, and cover every inch of their bare skin with a thick layer of hot grease. They would then pin their bound, naked, grease-covered captives to enormous ant hills. They would break the hills wide open, and let the ants do the rest.

The grease was like a magnet to the ants, and drawn to it like moths to a flame, thousands upon thousands of aggressive, opportunistic ants would cover the humans from head to toe and begin to feast. But those hungry ants didn't just eat the grease. They devoured all the flesh, too, until nothing remained but bone.

In other words, captives were eaten alive. And many settlers lost their lives to this unimaginable fate.

Young Francis ultimately survived capture. Out of fear, George and Sarah hid their son over the years, sometimes burying him beneath piles of laundry or under anything they could find. The unrelenting warriors, meanwhile, came and went without warning.

After managing to survive in the area for about a decade, John, George's brother, was killed during battle.

In 1853, shortly after John's passing, George had an unusual dream. A dream so vivid that he forever referred to it as a "manifestation."

In his journal, George suggests that he was out finishing his farm work for the day when he had an experience that blurred the line between fiction and reality. As the sun began to dip down into the background, George heard a strange voice shout his name. He turned around and saw an unfamiliar, angelic-like figure draped in all white.

The figure described two men who would show up at his home with a message of faith for George and his family. He would not know these men, but he was to heed their message. He was encouraged to treat them as friends, not strangers, and to listen to, accept, and act upon their words—no matter how outlandish the words may be.

Because George was a man of faith, and this "manifestation" appeared so real to him, he was completely convinced that those two messengers would one day arrive.

The story goes that, although Sarah admired her husband's unwavering faith, as time ticked on, she began to wonder aloud if George's dream was just that: a dream and only a dream.

That is, until the messengers arrived.

The men were exactly as they had been described to George. The message they shared was that of hope and faith. And their message compelled George to move his family yet again. This time, west. Far west.

To an entirely new continent. For a new life. And new land. Land that lay yet *another* eight thousand miles away. In North America.

After years of on-again, off-again war, George and Sarah had finally settled into their new home and new lives in Africa. Their first eight-thousand-mile trek was more than enough adventure to last a lifetime. They were lucky to be alive. Lucky only one family member had been taken from them. And now, George was to listen to complete strangers and embark on another impossible journey for what appeared to be an eerily similar opportunity? Last time, he led his family right into a deadly war. Why risk it all again? Why believe what could potentially be yet another empty promise?

My friend, what do you think George did?

What would you do?

George still had that unwavering hope, courage, and resilience he had when he first left England more than a decade earlier. He was still eager to pursue a better life for his family—which now included four more children in addition to Francis. George believed the message of the angelic-like figure who had lit up the night sky, as well as that of the two messengers who knew him by name. He believed that if the Princes could conquer the restless waters of the Atlantic Ocean—and survive yet another painstaking journey to a destination worlds away—a better life awaited his growing family.

So, the Princes traversed that untamed ocean. They docked along the east coast of the young United States of America, and in 1855, with no time to recover from yet another treacherous journey, the Princes hopped aboard the last wagon train of the season, which was destined to roll across the Great Plains and into Utah. This wagon train was headed to the very place the messengers had described to George.

For the Princes, what appeared to be a better, safer life was no longer an entire ocean away. Now, only a cross-country wagon trip separated George and his family from their new life and new land.

Unfortunately, what was supposed to be the final leg of their family's journey turned out to be its deadliest.

In the confined quarters of the cramped, covered wagon, Sarah delivered twins. But neither of the babies survived, both dying shortly after birth.

George and Sarah buried the newborns themselves. They had no choice but to leave their tiny bodies in an unmarked grave somewhere in the Great Plains— somewhere they would never see again.

Eventually the Princes arrived in Utah. But shortly after crossing into the territory, death struck again. Sarah died, never having reached their final destination. George would need to raise their family without her.

By this time, George Prince had lost his brother, two children, and now his beloved wife. Yet he pressed on for the sake of his five remaining children, Francis and the four others born to George and Sarah in Africa.

After traveling from England to Africa, Africa to Massachusetts, and Massachusetts to the Utah territory, George Prince finally reached his ultimate destination, the southern area of Utah. He had traveled approximately nineteen thousand miles, amounting to just over three quarters of the way around the Earth!

The Princes found faith, freedom, and happiness in Utah, in an area not far from where Isaac and I stood honoring George on that Memorial Day morning, more than one hundred years after the journey that led our ancestors here. And to a place where my family and I have found faith, freedom, and happiness too. It's a place we wouldn't be had it not been for George Prince. And history shows his trip was worth it. The Xhosa Wars continued, and even escalated, not long after George and his family left Africa. Had they stayed, the young Prince children could have been targets for the ruthless warriors and opportunistic ants. More death, despair, and heartbreak, almost guaranteed.

I often think about George. His hope, courage, and resilience. How his decisions have impacted my own family five and six generations later.

George had traveled across the world in search of a place for future generations of Princes to thrive. He lost a brother. He lost children. He lost his wife. He experienced death and disease firsthand. He tiptoed, unarmed, onto a bloody battlefield. Traversed entire oceans. And made unimaginable sacrifices along the way.

He did all of this for his children. He did it for their children. And, I believe, he did it for me and my children. That's why five generations later, I feel a deep connection with George, a unique bond, even a great debt to him. So much so, it makes me emotional at times. The sacrifices he made to give his family a better life, in turn, gave me and my family a better life.

Think about that for a second.

Do you realize that even the smallest decisions you make today affect the future of your family tomorrow . . . and beyond?

Your decisions directly affect your descendants. Your children. Their children. Even children related to you who will come five and six generations from now.

The hope, courage, and resilience that remained with George through death and despair are gifts that have been passed down our family line, generation by generation, to me and my children.

George changed our family tree forever. That's not lost on me nor on Isaac. We won't let it be. He was *that* person for our family. And I believe you have the opportunity to be that person for your family.

In fact, I believe you have that obligation. I believe you've been given that gift. You are not here by accident. And the truth is, you have had an entire heritage of people who have lived and bled and died for you, so that you can have this moment to do something great and be something great.

For you to be born, twelve generations, 4,094 of your ancestors, your flesh and blood, came together from all over the world to create you. Think about that. Think about them.

How many sacrifices did they make? How many battles did they face? How many tears did they shed? How much hurt did they endure? How much joy did they experience? How much hope did they have? How much suffering did they struggle through?

Think about what thousands of your ancestors endured for you to have the gift of life, to be here at this very moment.

They are not just names etched on a tombstone. They are people. People who faced struggles similar to what George, Sarah, John, and Francis faced.

They fought. They cried. They bled. They loved. They lived. They laughed. For you.

Without them, there *is* no you.

They gave you this moment.

My point is, your life isn't random. Your life isn't the result of luck, chance, or coincidence. Your life has purpose. It has value and meaning. It's been said that the odds of being born are one in 400 trillion. Just by being here, reading this, you won the lottery . . . many times over. And you were put here with a mission. You were put here to "be the one." To "be the one" who lives a life and writes an unforgettable story for your family tree, which enables future generations to look up and say:

"It was him."

"It was her."

"He's 'the one.'"

"She's 'the one.'"

He's "the one" who altered the pattern of abuse. She's "the one" who overcame the addiction. He's "the one" who ended our financial struggles. She's "the one" who snapped generational chains.

He's "the one" who started the business. She's "the one" who built the empire. He's "the one" who left the inheritance. She's "the one" who planted new roots. He's "the one" who set the example. She's "the one" who inspires us.

And they're telling *your* story.

That list could go on with all kinds of monumental accomplishments. But do you know how many people it takes to do all these things?

One.

Just one person can change the family tree forever.

My friend, be that one person. "Be the one."

You see, I'm not encouraging you to *become* "the one" or *grow into* "the one" or *develop into* "the one." I'm encouraging you to "*be* the one." I use the word *be* because you already are "the one."

It's not just *in* you. It *is* you.

You're "the one" your ancestors lived, bled, and died for. You're "the one" whom 4,094 people came together to create. And you're "the one" whom entire generations of your descendants are counting on to live an unforgettable life.

Imagine five and six generations from now, your young grandson or your granddaughter, kneeling at your grave to thank you for being "the one."

Benjamin Franklin once wrote, "If you were not to be forgotten as soon as you are dead and rotten, either write things worth reading or do things worth writing."[1] This book will help you "be the one" who does something worth writing *and* reading.

In the coming pages, I will share stories that will inspire you, move you, and motivate you. But we won't stop there. This isn't just another motivational book. Motivation isn't enough to "be the one."

Instead, I will hand you the tools, reveal the habits, and guide you through the precise steps and strategies for you to "be the one." Legendary poet Ralph Waldo Emerson has been quoted as saying, "The only person you are destined to become is the person you *decide* to be."

It's your decision.

The word *decision* contains the suffix -*cision*, which comes from Latin and means "to cut." So -*cision* means "cut," and *de-* means "off."

An *incision* cuts in, but a *decision* cuts off. When you make a decision, you *cut off* all other possibilities.

"Be the one" who does something worth writing *and* reading.

Make the decision now to pick up the proverbial pen of your life. To write a life story that your descendants will remember and retell. To live a life that changes your family tree forever. And to cut off all other possibilities.

Before you read on, make the decision to "be the one."

1

Create and Design Your Future

Nobel Prize–winning playwright George Bernard Shaw said, "Life isn't about finding yourself. Life is about creating yourself." In other words, we are creators.

Even the Bible speaks to this. The very first line of the Old Testament is dedicated to it. It reads, "In the beginning, God created the heaven and the earth."

Regardless of your religion or what you believe, think of all the ways that God could have been introduced: as the Father, the Almighty, the Lord, or the Divine.

Yet, he is introduced as what?

As a—or the—Creator.

The visionary cofounder of Apple, Steve Jobs, is quoted as saying, "Everything around you that you call life was made up by people that were no smarter than you. And you can change it, you can influence it, and you can build your own things that other people can use. So don't just live a life, build one."

The essence of his message is this: We are all builders. Creators. And get this—Steve Jobs didn't believe in God in the conventional sense. He was a self-proclaimed Buddhist.

You see, our role as creators transcends religion. But it also transcends time.

In 2022, Dubai's Museum of the Future, dubbed "the most beautiful building in the world," opened its doors. This museum is an otherworldly structure that would leave iconic creators from Shaw to Disney to Jobs to Musk in awe. It looks like a glamourous and gigantic marbled ring comfortably resting on its side for all to admire. And the stunning creation's exterior is decorated to be one thing: an ode to humanity's role as creators. Colossal Arabic calligraphy blankets the high-tech architectural wonder, which translates to, "We may not live for hundreds of years, but the products of our creativity can leave a legacy long after we're gone," and "The future belongs to those who can imagine it, design it, and execute it. It is not something you await, it's something you create."

© Museum of the Future

So no matter the source, be it the words of the Bible, the assessment of a visionary, or a modern ode to the future, they all say the same thing: We are all creators. We were put on Earth to imagine, design, execute, build . . . and create.

Now, maybe you've never considered yourself a creator before. Maybe you don't consider yourself a creator now. Perhaps you feel that creating is better suited for someone else. Someone smarter or stronger or more successful. Maybe creation seems like a special power, gift, or talent reserved only for others.

Honestly, I can relate to that feeling.

Before I recognized my power to create, I began listening to a renowned personal development seminar that the great Jim Rohn, Tony Robbins's first mentor, recorded back in 2004. It was an iconic Rohn event, an event that all the greats of the time attended, which is why the audio was captured on a series of CDs long before audiobooks were "a thing." I vividly remember protecting those CDs from collecting even a single scratch, like they were as important as my life. To this day, I can still hear Rohn's familiar voice pumping through my old, white Toyota Corolla.

One of the most powerful and unforgettable things Jim Rohn said came at the very end of the event, on the final day, after all of the greatest speakers of the time had shared their success stories with an eager audience of hundreds, if not thousands. Rohn closed the event slowly and deliberately sharing this wisdom: "From these testimonials and from these personal experiences we have enough information to conclude that it is possible to create and design an extraordinary life."

He said that "it is possible to *create* and *design* an extraordinary life."

To me, it was a reminder, or a declaration, that we are creators. That I could be a creator. That I *am* a creator.

But I still remember thinking, *I know it's possible for all of those people to create and design an extraordinary life . . . but is it really possible for me?*

You know how it is. You see and hear others' success stories. But self-doubt, skepticism, and cynicism creep in. Maybe *your* challenges and circumstances are unique. Maybe you have fewer resources to draw from.

Perhaps luck isn't on your side. Or a completely different set of cards are stacked against you. You could flip through an endless Rolodex of excuses, or reasons, as to why you can't be like them.

Despite Rohn's words and the many testimonials and experiences shared by the other speakers, as well as plenty of "regular" people in the crowd, I still found myself wondering, even debating, if success was possible for *me*. And I'll tell you why: like you, I've had my own challenges to overcome.

I come from a broken home. My parents divorced when I was twelve years old. We moved thirteen times over the next seven years. I dropped out of college before finishing my freshman year. I worked construction for my dad, flipped pizzas for a friend's dad, and sold animated Bible videos from a mall kiosk. My education is limited, and my professional experience wasn't much to write home about.

Despite all that, I still had big dreams. So at twenty-five years old, with little experience and education to rely on, I started my very first business.

I wanted to live a significant life. I wanted to chase my dreams. I wanted to make my son, Isaac, my daughter, Ciera, and my wife, Missy, proud of me.

And guess what?

The business failed. I burned right through my savings. We had to live on credit cards, and we fell behind on our taxes. My big dream was a colossal failure, which left my family and me not just broke, but below "zero" financially.

We were forced to move in with Missy's parents just to make ends meet. My wife, my son, my daughter, and I shared a one-bedroom loft above their garage. Plus, we had another family member on the way. Missy was pregnant with our third child, Lexi.

Imagine raising a family of four in a single bedroom . . . at your in-laws. The space was so small that Isaac and Ciera slept in the closet. I was disappointed. Discouraged. Even defeated. I balled like a baby the night I knew my business was officially over, all because I felt like I'd let my family down. How dare I think success was possible for me. Who did I think I was to create and design an extraordinary life?

Since my résumé didn't scream success, I took the only jobs I could get, two of them, both part-time. Once again, I was selling animated Bible videos on the weekends. From the mall kiosk, from the pavement of parking lots, at fairs, at events, and beyond. And then, each weekday, I'd knock on doors to try and sell—get this—twenty-five-year emergency food storage containers.

That's what you call living the dream, right? Forget possible. At that point, Jim Rohn's declaration felt impossible to me.

Maybe it seems impossible for you too. Maybe right now, your dreams and goals seem impossible.

Well, seventeen years after first hearing Rohn's words, I can tell you, based on *my own* testimonial and *my own* personal experience, that it *is* possible. It is possible for you to create and design an extraordinary life. It is possible for you to create and design the future that you want—no matter what the present looks like.

You see, I regained enough courage to start another business shortly after. To believe in myself again. To chase my dream again. But my struggle was far from over. I went back to working both part-time jobs, on top of starting my new, second business. Over time, that business allowed me to finally leave one job and then the other. That little business grew into my full-time thing. And thanks to its success, I sold that business a number of years later. Armed with new resources, relationships, and experiences, I had the opportunity to help a private equity firm do the impossible—to turn around a rapidly declining twenty-five-year-old company that had experienced double-digit-per-year declines in revenue for, get this, eight straight years. This business was a behemoth, generating a few hundred million a year in revenue and operating across twenty-five countries around the world, yet it was sinking as fast as the Titanic.

As I learned from my personal experience, the two hardest things to do in business are a start-up and a

I can tell you, based on *my own* testimonial and *my own* personal experience, that it *is* possible. It is possible for you to create and design an extraordinary life.

turnaround. So we decided the best course of action was to do both . . . at once. We stripped the business down to the floorboards. Then we treated it like a new company, like a start-up. The business was in business, yet we changed everything. And when I say everything, I mean everything. We created a new name. We designed a new business model. We built new products. Introduced new leadership. New systems. New comp plans. Everything was new, new, new. Yet we couldn't afford to lose our old, or existing, customers. It was like we were changing the engine of a hulking 737 while flying at thirty thousand feet. And guess what? We did it. And it worked. That business skyrocketed. It went from barely surviving to thriving. Since then, I've helped that same business generate more than 2.4 billion dollars in sales and acquire more than four million customers. Plus, I've built my own multimillion-dollar businesses. Five of them.

My point is, after my very first failure, I didn't give up. I didn't stop dreaming. I didn't stop believing. I didn't stop creating. And after several more years of striving, working, planning, praying, sacrificing, and struggling, I found myself creating and designing an extraordinary future. My big dreams became my reality. And now I'm living an extraordinary life.

I've been invited to tell my story in more than thirty countries around the world. And I've shared stages with

After my very
first failure,
I didn't give up.
I didn't stop
dreaming.
I didn't stop
believing. I didn't
stop creating.

icons like John C. Maxwell, Jamie Kern Lima, and Ed Mylett, to name a few.

And it bears repeating, because it's *that* important—I can tell you now, with 100 percent certainty, that it is possible for you to create and design an extraordinary life.

Because like me, you are a creator. Regardless of your roots. Your background. Your education. Your experience. Your resources. Or your lack thereof. Like Shaw, like Jobs, like Rohn, like Robbins, and like so many others—names you know and names you don't—I know this to be true from my personal experience and my testimonial. I now know that what is possible for one is possible for many.

Don't turn the page without recognizing and embracing who you really are: a creator. And like me, you have the power to create and to design the life that, right now, you may only be able to imagine. In the following pages, I will show you how to do just that.

"Be the one" who creates and designs an extraordinary life.

CHAPTER

2

Live an Intentional Life

In search of inspiration after a particularly discouraging week at work when my commission totaled zero, I slid a different CD into my car stereo. It was the audio from John C. Maxwell's *New York Times* bestselling book *The 21 Irrefutable Laws of Leadership*. And as soon as I pressed play, it was as if John was speaking directly to me—and *only* me.

Have you ever felt that way? Have you ever heard a story, speech, or message that seemed almost tailor-made for you at that very moment?

It was as if John were riding shotgun with me. Coaching me up as my copilot from the brown cloth interior of my rundown Corolla. In fact, I chose to take the long way home that night to give myself more time with John and to soak in his timely message. And during that extended drive home, I went from feeling bad for myself and my situation to suddenly feeling empowered, confident, even free. That trip home inspired me to get my hands on every John C. Maxwell book that I could find. And since he's written more than one hundred books, I had options.

But I didn't stop there.

I began studying and dissecting his speeches, line by line, word by word. I was instantly a fan. I still am. And it's almost surreal for me to share this, but since that time, John has also become a personal friend and mentor. Talking face-to-face—well, that's the ultimate experience.

I've sat in his home office, in his den, where he's penned many of those award-winning books. I've shared dinner with him and his wife, Margaret, at their dining table. And as I mentioned earlier, I've spoken on the same stages as he has, at events no different than the ones Jim Rohn used to host.

I've even had the privilege of traveling with John and a small group of his closest confidants to facilitate "country transformations," where we teach critical leadership principles to people in underserved communities. It was during a "transformation" in Costa Rica that John revealed the "one thing" that changed my life. And as we continue our journey together, I believe this "one thing" will change yours too.

On that trip, we met with everyone from the US Ambassador to Costa Rica to the head of the international football/soccer federation (FIFA) to all kinds of local business leaders, meeting many of them at the country's famed National Theater. But, to my surprise, the most memorable moment was unexpectedly shared with hundreds of ordinary college students . . . students and teachers crammed inside a middling auditorium, standing room only, in a remote village.

That was where John shared four words that reveal *how* to create and design an extraordinary life. Four simple words, without which you can never "be the one." Those four words are: Live an intentional life.

You see, John has a unique speaking style. He doesn't rely on theatrics, props, power points, or anything else to command a room and compel the individuals in it. Instead, he sits on a tall chair on a bare stage and lets his words and wisdom do the refining.

So there John was, in a midnight blue blazer with his dark gray hair neatly combed back, perched atop the seat of a tall padded chair, flanked by his translator, Juan Vereecken, also known as JV. (You can think of JV as the Latin version of John Maxwell. His words, his actions, and even his mannerisms match John's to a tee.) The only thing separating the two seated men was a small table for John's iPad, his water bottle, and for his left elbow to rest upon. This was John's standard setup. Nothing new or unusual about it.

And there I was, looking up toward John from the audience, along with a small team of his personal friends and colleagues. We were surrounded by nearly five hundred young students who filled every seat, packing that intimate auditorium, all there eager to hear John speak. After all, this was a rare and thrilling opportunity to rub elbows with an American legend right in their own backyard.

But minutes into John's speech, something unusual happened.

Of all the speeches I'd carefully studied, dissected, and even attended, I'd never heard or seen John do something like this. In the middle of a sentence, he abruptly stopped speaking.

This wasn't a pause to take a breath or to swig some water. His words came to a screeching halt. Even JV seemed surprised.

Then John slowly leaned back into the padding of his chair, wrapped one leg over the other, and folded his arms. His eyebrows furrowed, he rested his left hand under his chin, reminiscent of Auguste Rodin's famed sculpture, *The Thinker.*

It was as if an illuminating thought had unexpectedly struck John, and he needed a moment to bottle it up before it disappeared. JV was a beat behind; he wrapped his own legs and folded his arms, but on a short delay, indicating this hadn't been rehearsed. John's body language did the only talking in that auditorium. It announced to the enthusiastic students that he was deep in thought. A message they understood, sans translation.

After a few seconds, John tilted forward toward the audience. He was ready to continue. We hoped he was ready to reveal what had stopped him in his tracks. Then he said, "If there was only one thing I could share with you that would have the most impact in your life, it would be this . . ."

It would be what?

You see, he didn't finish the sentence. *Again* he stopped speaking. He leaned back in his chair and returned to that thoughtful position from moments earlier. Perhaps he had to tie a bow on his thought before revealing that "one thing."

But after another moment or two of pure silence, John rose to his feet. Then he walked forward. Closer and closer to the students. Closer and closer to us.

He stopped at the very edge of the stage. Then he slowly raised his right arm up into the air. And held it high. He still hadn't finished his sentence. He simply stood there, silently, with his right hand raised to the sky.

Five seconds passed. Then ten. JV also rose to his feet, walked forward, and stood next to John. Like John, he, too, raised his right hand to the sky.

As the two men remained as still and silent as Rodin sculptures, I noticed several students scanning the room, their eyes filled with wonder, silently asking what was going on. Yet everyone in that auditorium seemed to understand that this was not theatrics. This was not manufactured drama. With his right arm held high, John was carefully considering his next words, the ones that would bring a close to this captivating cliffhanger.

Seconds felt like minutes as the silence continued. The sea of students around us remained captivated by curiosity. They couldn't wait to hear the "one thing."

To be honest with you, I was equally curious . . . and confused. I'd never seen John do anything like this. And as a fan-turned-friend, I thought I'd seen it all.

Then all of the sudden, one of the students, a young woman maybe eighteen years old, stood up and raised her right arm—just like John and JV. Seconds later, another student did the same thing; she stood and held her right arm in the air.

Then another. And another. One-by-one, then two-by-two, until students were rising up in clusters, all mimicking John's and JV's posture. Picture it: hundreds of students standing tall, with one arm in the air, as if a miracle was about to be performed directly in front of them.

Despite the movement, the stuffed auditorium remained silent. Yet anticipation pulsed through it like electricity.

I, too, was on my feet when John finally spoke: "If there's only one thing I could share with you that would have the most impact on your life, it would be this . . ."

Then he revealed his "one thing."

Those four simple words: "Live an intentional life."

Looking up toward his right hand, John continued, "All of success is all uphill all the way. Most people have uphill hopes and downhill habits. You don't accidentally go up hills. You only intentionally go up hills." And then he repeated it: "So . . . live an intentional life."

That was it. John's "one thing." Just four simple words. No hour-long monologue. No lengthy supporting story or speech. No special guests, no cameras, and no reason to perform. John simply gifted those students his most life-changing advice at the very moment it hit him.

That was the "one thing" that stopped the world's foremost authority on leadership smack dab in the middle of a speech he'd given hundreds of times. *Live an intentional life.*

But can I tell you something? Those four words are more powerful to me than any of the other stories I've

Most people
have uphill
hopes and
downhill habits.
You don't
accidentally
go up hills.

heard, words I've read, speeches I've dissected, and conferences I've attended.

In his bestselling book *The Monk Who Sold His Ferrari*, author Robin Sharma says, "Never overlook the power of simplicity." John's "one thing," which amounted to four words, is equally simple, powerful, and profound. Maybe even *magical*, at least for me.

What about you?

Allow those words to stop you for a moment. Allow the "one thing" to sink in. Allow it to move you. On the surface, I understand it may not seem like much.

Live an intentional life.

Perhaps it seems too simple. Maybe even easy to overlook. So, let's dig deeper.

Are you living an intentional life?

Are you intentional in your pursuit of your goals and dreams? Are you intentional in your health? Are you intentional in your relationships? Are you intentional in your faith? Are you intentionally creating, building, and designing your future?

Or are you just floating through life? Drifting with the currents in whatever direction they pull you, allowing life to happen *to* you instead of *for* you?

Most people live in a world of reaction to distraction rather than a world of intentional creation. We react to the things that happen to us. We react to our notifications. We react to the news. The text messages. The emails. The reels. The videos. The violence. The headlines. And so on.

Reaction is the enemy of intention. It's the polar opposite. The opposing force. Reaction is no different than gravity. It pulls you down, preventing you from living an intentional life. And the uncomfortable truth is, reaction is our default setting. It's our norm, our status quo. We are essentially conditioned to react.

But all reaction does is steal years from your life and life from your years. Ironically, reaction is the "one thing" that stops us from doing the real "one thing": living an intentional life.

So, I want you to remember this: creation starts with intention. You can create and build and design your future *if* you live an intentional life.

But first, make the decision to leave the life of reaction and to live a life of intention. A life of creation. Make the decision now to do the "one thing."

"Be the one" who lives an intentional life.

You can create and build and design your future *if* you live an intentional life.

CHAPTER
3

Update Your Identity

In the *New York Times* bestselling book *Atomic Habits: Tiny Changes, Remarkable Results*, author James Clear shares the story of two boys who were asked the same question: "Who stole the candy?"

The first boy snapped back, "I did not steal the candy." Then the second boy calmly stated, "I do not steal."

Do you see the difference in their responses? It's subtle yet significant.

"I did not steal the candy" is an action. "I do not steal" is an identity.

Success, too, is an identity process, because you will never outperform the way you see yourself. If you see yourself as a loser, you won't play like a winner. If you see yourself as a winner, you won't quit like a loser.

Over time, we are all consistent with our identity. So, what is your identity?

What comes to mind when I ask you that question? Chances are you've never thought about your identity. Have you? You probably didn't know you can—or need—to update it. And perhaps your own self-limiting beliefs are preventing you from making the update required to "be the one."

Don't make the mistake of thinking your identity cannot change. That success is for someone else, someone different. And don't think that somehow your past failures, struggles, insecurities, or challenges require you to cling to an outdated identity.

Don't make the mistake that so many of us do of thinking you are stuck with, or anchored to, an old identity.

My friend Jaime (pronounced HIE-me) Molina—a name you've probably not heard alongside Rohn, Maxwell, or Jobs—serves as a counselor for struggling youth and families in his local Southern California community. And he's the perfect guy for that job.

Jaime's a kind, gentle, and generous family man. He's a father to four daughters. A loyal husband of more than thirty-four years. An El Paso, Texas, native who radiates warmth from his round, welcoming face, kind brown eyes, and spiked salt-and-pepper hair. If you ask me, he's the kind of person you want your kids to grow up to be like. That's why I'm proud to call him a friend.

To inspire the young men and women he counsels, Jaime often shares the story of a man he once knew. This man was not known by his name, but a number: E90400.

At the tender age of eight, alcohol became a recurring part of E90400's life. At nine years old, he was molested by someone twenty years his senior. He was exposed to drugs at just fourteen years old. He found they helped dull the unfortunate blend of hunger pangs and hopelessness he battled as a teen. By fifteen years old, E90400 was hooked on heavy drugs. Before he could legally place his hands on the wheel to drive a car, he was already a "mule" for local drug runners. He flunked out of high school. And as you can imagine, things only continued to get worse for E90400.

In his late twenties, he was charged with eleven different felonies and was sentenced to forty-four months in prison. But not just any prison. He was shackled up and sent to California's infamous San Quentin State Prison, one of America's most notorious and dangerous maximum-security correctional facilities, known for harsh living conditions, violence, and overcrowding.

It was there this man became known as E90400.

Those six characters were his inmate ID. In other words, they were his identity.

Now here's where things get really interesting. After sharing the story of E90400, Jaime always asks the group, "What do you think happened to E90400?"

What do you think happened to the little boy who started drinking in the third grade? The tender child who was molested and sexually active by the fourth grade? The kid who was hooked on hard drugs by his freshman year of high school? The young man locked in an unforgiving, overcrowded cell alongside murderers, rapists, and the most dangerous and violent criminals in the state?

Do you think E90400 is still behind bars? Serving life in prison? Living on the streets? Is he dead? Is he dealing?

These are all logical outcomes. Expected outcomes.

After his audience blurts out their predictions, Jaime asks a follow-up question: "Would you like to know what happened to E90400?"

The kids nod.

"Would you like to meet E90400?"

They nod again.

Then Jaime asks a crazier question: "Would you like to meet him right now?"

You can almost see their jaws graze the ground. The kids are bewildered. Surprised. Excited. Perhaps a tad scared. They again nod in unison.

Turns out the man known as E90400 is no longer locked behind bars. He's not living on the streets. And he hasn't experienced the afterlife yet. Believe it or not, he's actually in the hallway. "Should I grab him?" Jaime asks.

With their approval, Jaime slips out of the room to invite E90400 in. He closes the door behind him. And shuffles down the hallway.

The wide-eyed youth eagerly await Jaime's return with E90400. Nobody says a word. They're fixated on that door.

Who is E90400? What is he doing here? How could he even be here?

Seconds later, the door handle turns. The room goes silent. Jaime cracks the door open, peeks his head in, and scans the room to confirm everybody's ready. He can almost feel the suspense in the air. Then Jamie slowly steps back into the room.

But wait.

He's alone.

The puzzled students stare. They crane their necks to look down the hallway.

Where's E90400?

Jaime takes a deep breath.

Then says, "I was E90400."

What?

The kids can't comprehend his words. At times I can't either. Jaime, the near perfect family man guiding today's youth down a better path, perhaps the kindest man I've ever met, and the husband to perhaps the kindest woman I've ever met, was E90400.

He's the boy who was exposed to booze and sexually molested before graduating grade school. The troubled teen hooked on drugs and working for dealers before flunking out of high school. The young man who spent what should have been his best years behind bars in America's toughest prison.

Jaime is that boy who had been to proverbial hell and back before most of us even met our significant other, got our own health insurance, or landed our first full-time job.

It turns out, he was telling his story.

The man formerly known as E90400 now has four daughters. He has been happily married for more than three decades. He makes an honest living in financial services. And he gives back to his community by serving as a counselor and agent of change to young men and women facing similar challenges as he did, challenges that led him down the wrong road.

If you met Jaime, you'd never know these things about him. You'd never guess it.

E90400 is not who Jaime is. E90400 is who he was.

He went from E90400 to Jaime Molina.

He updated his identity. And you can do the same.

Jaime is proof that your past is not predictive. You are not your mistakes. You are not your missteps. You are not your divorce. You are not your bankruptcy. You are not your abuse. You are not your addiction. You are not the girl with body issues. You are not the boy who was bullied. And so on and so forth.

You are not who you *are*. You are who you were born to be.

Let me reiterate: You are "the one."

But to "be the one," you must update your identity. Like E90400 did.

The famous Greek philosopher Socrates has been quoted as saying, "The secret of change is to focus all of your energy on not fighting the old, but on building the new." But here's the challenge: updating your identity to build a new you isn't as simple as updating your cell phone, because we often feel tethered to our current identity. And our current identity tends to be how others have defined us. They've told us who we are and who we should be. They've shaped and formed our identity for us. So even when you desperately want to make an update, it can be hard to overcome the lies, myths, misconceptions, and opinions others have led you to believe about yourself.

I'll give you an example.

A boy named Leslie Brown and his twin brother, Wesley, were born out of wedlock on the cold, cement floor of an abandoned warehouse in Miami's low-income Liberty City neighborhood. When the baby

But here's the challenge: updating your identity to build a new you isn't as simple as updating your cell phone, because we often feel tethered to our current identity.

boys were given up by their biological mother, they were adopted by a strong black woman with a bright white smile that could light up any room . . . a woman named Mamie Brown.

Mamie loved those boys like her own and set them up for success by ensuring they received an education.

But little Leslie struggled in school. So much so that, by the fifth grade, he was labeled "educable mentally retarded," a psychological term for someone who can still function but has a lower-than-average IQ. He was sent back to repeat the fourth grade. And from his second go-round as a fourth grader all the way to his junior year of high school, Leslie was a mainstay in special education classes. It seemed that's where he belonged.

Then one afternoon in the eleventh grade, Leslie ventured inside an unfamiliar classroom to meet a friend. The bell rang, indicating the start of class, but Leslie's friend was nowhere to be found among the students, now seated and looking at Leslie in the front of the room. Leslie turned to leave. But just as his hand grazed the door handle to exit into the hallway, the teacher behind him gave him an unexpected assignment.

From behind his desk, Mr. LeRoy Washington called to Leslie and pointed to the forest green chalkboard blanketing the main wall of the classroom.

"Young man," he said, "go to the board and work out this problem for me."

Leslie hesitated, so the teacher repeated his directive.

"I can't do that, sir" Leslie said politely.

"Why not?" Mr. Washington asked.

Leslie explained that he was just there hoping to catch his friend. "I'm not one of your students," he said.

"It doesn't matter," the teacher said. "Work on the problem anyhow."

Leslie again declined. "I can't do that, sir."

The rest of the students grew restless from their seats. Mr. Washington sensed they knew something that he didn't.

Then a young lady chimed in from the front row. "Mr. Washington," she said. "He's Leslie. He's got a twin brother, Wesley. Wesley's the smart one! Leslie is the DT."

Caught off-guard, Mr. Washington asked, "What's DT?"

The students began to snicker from their seats.

Leslie grew uncomfortable. He was aware he was about to be exposed—his greatest weakness about to be revealed, and from the very front of the classroom for everyone to see. His heart pounded. He gripped his backpack straps so hard his palms began to burn. He dropped his head to protect himself from the humiliating sight of his peers.

The girl in the front row seemed almost excited to offer her teacher an explanation. "He's the DT," she said. "The *Duuumb* Twin!"

The room erupted. Leslie, meanwhile, was stuck front and center. Paralyzed by embarrassment.

But this was no laughing matter to Mr. LeRoy Washington.

To the teacher's surprise, Leslie didn't deny the accusation. In fact, he affirmed the young lady's unfortunate assessment. "I am, sir," he said as he stared at his feet. "I'm educable mentally retarded."

Mr. Washington sprang up from his chair, rounded the corner of his desk, and bee-lined it to Leslie. He looked deep into the young man's chestnut brown eyes, which were welling with tears. Then he spoke to him as if they were the only two people in the packed classroom. "Don't you ever say that again, son." Like a father sharing wisdom that would last a lifetime, he said, "Someone's opinion of you does *not* have to become your reality."[2]

As Leslie digested those words, tears streamed down his cheeks. But they were not tears of embarrassment. They were tears of *joy*. He was crying because, in that moment, he went from humiliated to liberated.

"They said I was slow, so I held to that pace," Leslie would recount years later. He had believed he was educable mentally retarded, so it became his identity. Leslie was the "DT." But LeRoy Washington's wise words liberated Leslie from that identity. They gave him the nudge he needed to update his identity.

What do you think happened to Leslie Brown?

Well, you may know Leslie as Les. And Les Brown is one of the most sought-after and respected keynote speakers in the world. *Fortune* 500 organizations like McDonald's, IBM, and AT&T battle for his time. Success, Inc., NBC, and Toastmasters have showered him with prestigious accolades and awards. Les Brown is a former member of the Ohio House of Representatives, a bestselling author, and has been a syndicated broadcaster and television host.

That's right. That "retarded" boy is a modern-day renaissance man.

But why? And how?

Because he updated his identity.

My friend, someone's opinion of you does *not* have to become your reality. It does not have to be your identity. You can decide today to update your identity. To grow into the person you were born to be. As Les would say, "The way we live our lives is the result of the story we believe about ourselves."[3]

You're not your proverbial E90400. You're not your proverbial "DT." You are not the names and labels people have given you—nor the names and labels you've placed upon yourself.

Someone's opinion of you does *not* have to become your reality. It does not have to be your identity.

Imagine if Jaime still saw himself as E90400. Imagine if Les still saw himself as the "DT." Imagine if these men never updated their identities.

Let's begin to update your identity together. Right here, right now. Let me walk you through a simple two-step exercise to make the update. Because my guess is this is long overdue.

Step 1. Choose three aspirational words that describe your future best self.

Think of these as three words that describe your future identity, three words you want to be associated with you. Not who you are, but who you want to be. Words you'd like to emulate. You can even think of these as words you'd like others to use to describe you.

Here are some examples: Resilient. Patient. Inspiring. Understanding. Courageous. Confident. Competent. Mature. Thoughtful. Ambitious. Focused. Bold.

What words will you choose? Write them in the space below. Those three words are the starting point to update your identity.

_____

_____

_____

Step 2. Lean into those three words.

Act as if you are those three words from this moment forward.

Don't become them, be them.

How would someone who personifies those three words act? How would they live their life? How would they respond to adversity? How would they speak? How would they think? What would they do? What wouldn't they do? Answer these questions in the space below. In other words, bring those three words to life with context.

_____

_____

_____

_____

_____

Now treat those three words as your new identity. Forget the old. And be the new. This exercise is easy, but the execution is hard. Commit yourself now to be that person. And from this day forward, "be the one" who is resilient. "Be the one" who is patient. "Be the one" who is inspiring. And so on. It's in the doing that the "update" occurs.

"Be the one" who updates their identity.

CHAPTER

4

Clarify Your "3D" Vision

Every success story begins with vision. Your story is no different.

That's why all successful people, from Martin Luther King Jr. to Walt Disney, were lauded for their vision.

Have you ever stopped and asked yourself, "What is *my* vision? What do I really want to do with my life?"

Years ago, I worked with a man whose parents met while imprisoned at Auschwitz. Yes, *that* Auschwitz. The symbol of the Holocaust. A brutal complex that was home to forty-eight concentration and extermination camps. The place that stole more than one million innocent lives through inhumane beatings, burning, gassing, and torture.

My friend's parents were not sent to Auschwitz for being Jewish. In fact, they weren't even Jewish. They were each imprisoned simply for *showing sympathy* to the Jewish people who were being persecuted around them. And once there, they were treated just like every other prisoner in the camps.

Nearly nine out of ten people who entered Auschwitz never left. Think about that. My friend's parents had about a 90 percent chance of dying there. That means, they had a meager 10 percent chance of surviving the war. Yet they did survive, they were two among the rare few.

But survival didn't mean they were unaffected. After the war, survivors were left with physical, mental, and emotional scars, which would plague them for the rest of their lives. Visible and invisible marks that could never be erased.

To make matters worse, the prisoners at Auschwitz were liberated in the dead of winter. They stepped barefoot through dead bodies, dried up blood, and at times, heavy snowfall, with nothing but a few threads of tattered rags to cover their bony shoulders and malnourished bodies. Those threads were their only possessions. They had no food, no fuel, no family, and of course, no home to return to.

The end of imprisonment at Auschwitz simply marked the beginning of life as a refugee.

Eventually, my friend's parents scrounged up enough money to get to Ellis Island in New York Harbor. They began new lives in their new country by starting a family. Although my friend and his four brothers understood hard times—they were raised in a cinder block apartment complex that had no running water—my friend understood little of his parents' grim past until he reached a certain age. When he could finally fully absorb their story, he was shocked. He asked his father the same question I'm sure you and I would ask: "Dad, how did you survive Auschwitz?"

His father would recount being beaten until he dropped to his hands and knees. He was flogged until pain flooded his body from head to toe. Everything went black, and he fell unconscious. No sights. No sounds. No smells. His senses completely vanished.

It was like he was lost in space without the single flicker of a star. But just when he thought he was entering the afterlife, something appeared.

A vision.

It was a vision of his *unborn* sons. "A vision of you," he would say. "I'd see *you*."

Every time, it was the same: "Do you want to know what kept me alive, son? It was you. That vision of you and your brothers is what kept me alive."

While many prisoners would hope, pray, and even beg for death, this man's vision ensured that he would survive. It was the reason he never gave up.

How powerful is that?

A while ago, this friend gave me a gift reminiscent of his parents' story. It's a wooden plaque with the words "Lead with Vision" engraved on it to remind me of something he always says: "When times are tough, lead with vision." That's what his father did. That's what he does. And that's what I encourage you, "the one," to do.

My friend, you are "the one" for your family and heritage. To "be the one" you must live and lead your life with vision.

So together, let's craft your "3D" vision. It's a vision that will pull you out of any darkness and propel you through the toughest of times.

"When times are tough, lead with vision."

CRAFTING YOUR "3D" VISION

The First "D"—Define Your Vision

In his bestselling book *High Performance Habits*, the world's number one high-performance coach, Brendon Burchard, identified vision as one of the top things that separates successful people, or high performers, from the average person.

According to Burchard, high performers can articulate their goals or their future or their vision in seven to ten seconds or fewer, while the average person may take two to three *minutes* to do so. Said differently, high performers can state what they want to achieve and why it matters to them, without delay.

Why?

I believe it's because their vision is clearly defined.

A clearly defined vision sits on the tip of your tongue, not in the back of your mind. Whereas an unclear vision hides in the back of your mind; you may have pieces of the puzzle, but they are disconnected. And an unclear, or disconnected vision, will not serve its purpose. Your vision must be a dominant thought and a burning desire—all the pieces fitting together just right.

What is your vision? What are your dreams? What are your goals? What is your burning desire? What is your dominant thought, and is it clearly defined?

High performers can state what they want to achieve and why it matters to them, without delay

The challenge with vision is that most of us never take the time to stop and think about what we want to accomplish. We spend more time scrolling on social media, watching television, or planning our next vacation or date night than we do intentionally working on our goals, our futures, and our lives.

So, to help you clearly define your vision, I'd like to guide you through an illuminating exercise that will force you to stop and think about what you want to accomplish now, and later. You've probably never done something like this before, because most of us have never taken the time to think like this. Or to dream like this. Or to even focus on our future. So this may be challenging for you. Maybe even uncomfortable.

That's okay.

Take as much time as you need to work through the following steps. To think, to dream, and to focus. This vision-building and clarifying exercise is worth it.

Step 1: Write down five things you have already accomplished that you are proud of.

Think about those five things and why you're proud of them. Maybe you graduated from high school or college. Maybe you finished a 5K or ran a marathon. Maybe you married the love of your life or landed a job or earned a promotion or launched a business or paid off your debt or bought a home. Maybe you raised a family. Or maybe you're raising a family right now. These all qualify as accomplishments.

1. _____

2. _____

3. _____

4. _____

5. _____

These five accomplishments are a reminder that you've done, or accomplished, hard things. They will give you the momentum, confidence, and conviction to open up your dreams as we move to the next step of defining your vision.

Step 2: Write down fifty things you would like to accomplish in the next ten years.

This is going to be far more challenging. But I'm here to guide you. You see, most of us can write three, four, or five things that we'd like to have, accomplish, or do. But fifty? That can be tough. Especially since you've never done this before.

Remember, most people will go their entire lives without thinking about—let alone writing down—what they want to accomplish. So, to give you the freedom to dream and fill the space below with fifty things, do this: imagine that anything you write down on paper will happen.

Let's pretend it's that easy. Don't judge your dreams right now. Just think, dream, and write. If you write it down, you'll get it, period.

And if you're still struggling to pinpoint fifty things you want to have, accomplish, or do, here are some helpful questions to open up your mind and invite you to dream: What would your dream home look like? What would it have? Are you driving the car you want to drive? Do you want a new watch? Or new shoes? What kind?

Think about your professional life. What do you want to accomplish in your business or career? What title, rank, or position do you want? How much money do you want to make?

What about your health? Your hobbies? If you could travel anywhere in the world, where would you go? Who would you want to go with?

Think outside yourself too. What experiences do you want to create for other people? Do you want a family? What do you want to do with them? Or for them? Who do you want to help? How do you want to serve?

Take your time. Step away. Go think if you need to. There's no need to rush through this. In fact, you shouldn't rush through this. Only when you've filled your page with fifty things, move to the next step so we can further clarify your vision.

1. _____
2. _____
3. _____
4. _____
5. _____
6. _____
7. _____
8. _____
9. _____
10. _____
11. _____
12. _____
13. _____
14. _____
15. _____
16. _____
17. _____
18. _____
19. _____
20. _____
21. _____
22. _____
23. _____
24. _____
25. _____

26. _____
27. _____
28. _____
29. _____
30. _____
31. _____
32. _____
33. _____
34. _____
35. _____
36. _____
37. _____
38. _____
39. _____
40. _____
41. _____
42. _____
43. _____
44. _____
45. _____
46. _____
47. _____
48. _____
49. _____
50. _____

Step 3: Write a 1, 3, 5, *or* 10 *next to each of the fifty items you listed.*

These numbers represent years, the years you estimate it'll take to accomplish each goal. How long will each individual goal take you? One year? Three years? Five years? Or ten years?

Don't worry about being exact here. These are only estimates. As you analyze each of those fifty things above, jot down the first number that comes to your mind.

Step 4: Total up your 1s, 3s, 5s, *and* 10s *below.*

Total each number up below. How many *1s* do you have? How many *3s, 5s,* and *10s?*

Total 1s: _____

Total 3s: _____

Total 5s: _____

Total 10s: _____

If you have a whole bunch of *1s* and *3s,* you have more short-term goals than long-term. Challenge yourself to think bigger and longer as you clarify your vision. And if you have a whole bunch of *5s* and *10s,* challenge yourself to think deeper about what you can accomplish within the next year or two or three.

This will round out your vision by ensuring that you have a mix of short-term and long-term goals to guide you, year after year. Each one is a piece of the puzzle. And collectively, they form your vision.

Step 5: Select and list your top three 1s *that you want to accomplish.*

You can't chase fifty things at once. So for now, I'd like you to focus on your short-term goals. Your *1s* and perhaps your *3s.* Circle the top three goals you want to go after, the top three that you most want to accomplish in the short-term. Now, if someone asks what your latest goal or vision is, the answer is on the tip of your tongue. And as you accomplish each, you'll always know what's next. As you'll see, *3s* will become *1s, 5s* will become *3s,* and so on.

_____

_____

_____

Can I tell you what you just did?

You just laid out your vision. In increments of one, three, five, and ten years. Plus, you've selected your top three goals—the pieces of the puzzle that make up your vision, and the things you should be most focused on now. My friend, you now have a clear vision.

Now that you've defined your vision, it's time to move to the second "D" of your "3D" vision. For the remainder of this chapter, and this exercise, I encourage you to focus on only your most pressing goal. After you do this once, it's like riding a bike. You can confidently revisit and repeat this process for any goal.

The Second "D"—Declare Your Vision

Declaring your vision is the process of taking public the critical pieces, or goals, of the vision you've defined in private.

This is a critical step that will begin to guide you from dreaming to doing. Because when you declare your vision to others, something almost magic-like happens: It makes your dreams real. It anchors them in. And it forces you to take action by putting your reputation and credibility on the line.

Let me share a personal story that reveals both the power and purpose of declaring your vision.

A few years ago, I was thriving in several ways. My marriage was great. My business was flourishing. My kids were happy and healthy. But something was off.

My fitness had slipped. So to get back on track, I signed up for a men's physique competition.

I wasn't trying to transform into The Rock. I enrolled in the competition simply because I knew I needed a goal to stay motivated and on track, or else nothing would change. I would slip back into bad habits as most of us do if I didn't have a specific goal that I was working toward.

Plus, between you and me, I wanted my kids to see me set a goal and work to *achieve* it. I liked that a fitness-related goal had an element of visibility. They could actually see the effort I put in as well as the results. And it was a *1*. Meaning, I wanted to accomplish it within one year.

So, I made the decision to go all in. I hired a coach to craft my diet and to design my workouts. I told my brother, Travis, that I was going to compete too. To my surprise, he said, "I'll do it with you."

Then I declared my vision publicly by sharing it on Facebook. Candidly, I didn't head to Facebook with this "3D" framework in mind. I wasn't necessarily "declaring" my vision. I was doing it more or less to create content. After all, I knew I was already all in.

I was a few weeks into training when I recognized the power of my declaration. I was locking up the house in the dark of night, and my wife was dead asleep, as were the kids. As I quietly tip-toed into the kitchen, there they were: a plate covered with chocolate chip cookies my daughters, Ciera and Lexi, had slid out of the oven just before bed.

As you can imagine, I was on a strict diet. I was basically living on chicken breasts, brown rice, and the full rainbow of veggies. So just the sight of those cookies made my stomach rumble, and the smell almost made me drool. I kid you not, by pure imagination, I could almost taste the perfect blend of gooey dough and decadent chocolate melting in my mouth.

I remember thinking, *Nobody will know, dude. You deserve it.*

I approached those cookies like a lion eyeing its prey, slowly inching closer to the plate, while remaining keenly aware of my surroundings.

What do you think I did?

What would you do?

As badly as I wanted to (I can still picture that plate of moonlit cookies enticing me now), I didn't have a single cookie. I didn't take a single bite or even sneak a single crumb.

Why?

Well, I wish I could say it was because I had defined my vision, and therefore, I was "all in." But that wouldn't be completely true.

The reason I didn't eat the cookies that night was because I had *declared* my vision. I'd made a commitment to my brother as well as to all the people who had joined me or seen me on Facebook. If my vision had remained all about me, an empty plate would have been stuffed in the back corner of the dishwasher by the time the kids woke up for school. And Dad would have had no clue about what happened to those cookies.

I now recognize that I didn't give in to this temptation because I had declared my vision to others. I could have easily cheated myself. But I couldn't justify cheating the people I'd declared my vision to. I couldn't live with the idea of making a public declaration and then letting my kids down. Or letting my brother down. Or letting down any one of the people who had witnessed my declaration.

That's why declaring your vision is the next step after defining it.

We oftentimes will do things for others that we won't do for ourselves. Replace those cookies with any obstacle, desire, or deterrent standing in the way of your vision or goal, and the result is the same. Your declaration is what will keep you committed.

My declaration is what kept me committed to my goal of competing in that men's physique competition. I walked across that stage in the absolute best shape of my life. And I left the event hugging three trophies, having earned third place in two divisions and fifth overall. But the real victory was in the doing. I had stuck to my diet, no matter how hollow and hungry I felt. I didn't sneak a single "cheat" meal that wasn't part of my meticulously designed and incredibly rigid nutrition plan. I didn't skip my cardio, even though I despise long runs. And I never missed a weightlifting session, even if it meant forcing myself out of my warm bed at 2:00 or 3:00 or 4:00 a.m. I can tell you right now none of that would have happened if I hadn't declared my vision.

The late, legendary artist Georgia O'Keeffe said, "You get whatever accomplishment you are willing to declare." Declare your vision. Don't keep it a secret. Don't hide it in private. Who can you share your vision with today? Your family? Your friends? Your followers? Your network? Use the space below to pinpoint the people you will share your vision with and the places where you will declare it.

_____

_____

_____

_____

_____

The Third "D"—Dedicate Your Vision

When Anne Mulcahy was appointed CEO of Xerox in 2001, she was thrust into what was called "the perfect storm."[4] Not only was Mulcahy a shocking choice for CEO, Xerox was also on the verge of bankruptcy. The company had recorded substantial losses for each of the previous six years. Heck, it'd already lost more than $273 million the previous year alone![5]

Xerox was a stunning $17+ billion in debt. Oh, and it was facing a crippling SEC investigation. And if that

You've defined your vision. Now declare it. Don't keep it a secret. Don't hide it in private.

wasn't enough, the company's stock sank a whopping 15 percent when Mulcahy was announced as CEO.[6]

Why?

Mulcahy had no prior experience as a CEO. Let alone the type of experience the typical "turnaround" CEO of the time had. Mulcahy didn't even have the usual, or expected MBA. She had an English degree. And her only professional experience was at Xerox, where she had launched her career as a saleswoman fresh out of college. In her twenty-four years with the company, she'd spent sixteen of them in sales and the rest in human resources.

Xerox's stock plummeted the day Mulcahy took over because there was no reason to believe in her. Yet Anne Mulcahy, often referred to as the "accidental CEO," is the woman who brought Xerox back from the brink of bankruptcy. The company went from losing nearly $300 million a year to earning more than $1 billion just about four years after she became CEO.[7] Mulcahy went from least likely to succeed to one of the most powerful women in all of corporate America. In 2008, she was voted "Chief Executive of the Year" by her peers and named one of America's Best Leaders by *U.S. News and World Report*, all for orchestrating Xerox's dramatic turnaround.[8]

But how did a saleswoman with nothing more than an English degree lead a multibillion-dollar business transformation amidst crushing debt, ludicrous losses, employee defections, unhappy customers, and disconcerting investigations?

When Mulcahy took over, she found herself constantly fielding an unusual and unexpected question from employees at every level. Instead of the typical questions she anticipated and prepared for like, "Are we even going to survive? Should I be looking for another job? Who's getting laid off next?" Mulcahy was asked, "What's Xerox going to look like after we turn this thing around?"

The employees wanted her to describe what life would be like after the company's turnaround. *Wow*, she thought. *These employees are as dedicated as me.* Even though Rome was burning, people wanted to know what the city of the future would look like.

Meanwhile, the *Wall Street Journal* and other publications were already writing Xerox's obituary. It seemed like every day there was a new headline—be it about bankruptcy, the SEC investigation, the company's perceived incompetence, you name it.

So, the "accidental CEO" did something unorthodox: she wrote a fictitious *Wall Street Journal* article, which she dated four years into the future. In it, she outlined the things Xerox hoped to accomplish over the next several years as though the company had already achieved them. It was written as if Xerox were being celebrated by its biggest critic at the time. Mulcahy went so far as to include performance metrics, quotes from analysts, revenue growth, technological advancements, and more specific details in the article.

Now she could *show* employees what Xerox would look like after the turnaround. That article was her vision of what she wanted the company to somehow become. In other words, penning it was her way of *defining* her vision. And then she *declared* it, by sending the article to every single Xerox employee. In turn, the team rallied around Mulcahy's vision.

By 2005, just four years later, which happened to be the same "publication date" of Mulcahy's fictitious article predicting Xerox's future, the vast majority of what Mulcahy outlined in that article had come true. The vision she'd defined and declared became reality.[9]

So how was Anne Mulcahy able to orchestrate such a dramatic and unlikely transformation?

It wasn't simply by putting pen to paper. I'd argue that the primary reason for her success was not just her vision, but her fierce *dedication* to it.

For example, when Mulcahy first took over, she personally met with each of Xerox's top one hundred executives with an unusual proposition. She let them know how dire Xerox's situation was and asked if they were prepared to commit. If not, they'd be awarded a generous severance package to resign.[10]

"I gave people a choice to make," she said. "Either roll up your sleeves and go to work, or leave Xerox. I can't waste time with anyone who doesn't buy in. And doesn't care about the corporation the same way I do."

She wanted to determine if they were, in her words, "totally about Xerox." Were they as dedicated as she was? Turns out, they were. Ninety-eight out of the one hundred executives stuck around.

The company's customers did too. Mulcahy once said, "I will fly anywhere to save any customer for Xerox." And she did. Sometimes flying to three separate locations in one day—simply to save a customer.

If that's not dedication, I don't know what is.

And there are plenty more stories just like these illustrating Mulcahy's steadfast dedication to her vision. Some have even joked she was so dedicated that she bled toner. But this 2008 headline summed it up best: "Xerox's success is a reflection of her dedication."[11]

My friend, that multibillion-dollar turnaround doesn't happen without complete and total dedication. Nor do the accolades Anne Mulcahy earned.

You have to define your vision. Declare your vision. Then roll your sleeves up, get to work, and be totally about your vision.

In other words, you must dedicate your life to it.

"Be the one" with "3D" vision.

CHAPTER

5

Build the 3 Cs of Success

et's begin moving closer to your vision . . . mentally *and* physically. Let me introduce you to the 3 "Cs" that will propel you forward: Confidence. Commitment. Competence.

Together, these 3 Cs form a loop. They are all connected because you can't have one without the others.

THE 3 "C'S" SUCCESS LOOP

And by creating any one of these things, you'll create more of these things.

Now allow me to show you how to "be the one" with confidence, commitment, and competence.

THE FIRST C: CONFIDENCE

Create Confidence

The foundation of your success is believing in yourself. Simply put, you can't expect others to believe in you if you don't believe in yourself. So, allow me to ask you a question.

How confident are you in yourself?

Years back, my oldest son was emptying out a storage closet in our basement. Throughout the day, he'd climb up the stairs weighed down by boxes and other forgotten items, which were taking up space and collecting dust. Somewhere near the back of the storage closet, he came across an aging, plastic bin packed with personal development books and materials, like CDs and other recordings, from various conferences and events I'd attended over the years.

When he showed me the box, I couldn't help myself. I began flipping through pages of books, notes, and slides that brought me back to an earlier chapter of my life. Nostalgia flooded my thoughts. As I read the pages, I could remember the speakers. Their faces. Their messages. Their personalities. But one particular notebook from one particular event stood out from the rest.

Truth be told, it was from an event I could barely afford a ticket to. This event was right at the time that my first business had failed. We were behind on our taxes, buried in credit card debt, and living with my in-laws. And for the first time in my life, rock bottom was probably within reach. Maybe only days away.

But I still went to the event. I charged the ticket to my credit card. And paging through my notes all those years later, I remember the exact feelings I had when seated among the crowd of thousands, searching for hope and inspiration while feeling like a total failure. I remember transitioning from admiring the presenters on stage to feeling almost resentful of their success around that time. I wondered: Is this even going to work for me? Am I chasing a fake dream? Am I being strung along by these experts and gurus? I even asked myself, *What am I doing here?*

Have you ever had that feeling when you see someone successful? Have you ever thought, I could never do what they've done? Have you ever wondered if this will actually work for you? Have you ever asked yourself if you're chasing a fake dream or being strung along?

I felt like a total imposter floating in a sea of successful people at that event. Yet there I was. Dutifully filling pages with notes.

Flipping through that notebook was like taking a cathartic trip down memory lane—or nightmare alley. A trip that ended on the last page, as a few wet tears began to drip from my eyes. Because there it was. A note I had scribbled to myself from a blue ballpoint pen on the very last page of this notebook. A note that brought me back to the most trying times of my life. It read, "I BELIEVE IN MYSELF."

That's it. A statement declaring that I believed in myself.

I think that note made me emotional because, looking back, I had no reason to believe in myself at that time. None. Yet I still wrote those words on that page. Said differently, I still had confidence. I still kept going. I still believed in myself, despite what felt like a mountain of failures staring me in the face. And like a song, movie, or memory that takes you back to a specific moment in time, I can trace those words back to when things started changing for the better in my life.

My belief in myself was the foundation to my success.

So, do you believe in yourself?

How much do you believe in you? Author and activist Helen Keller said, "Nothing can be done without hope and confidence." But hope alone is not a strategy. You can't *hope* to be confident. But you *can* create confidence. Even if you feel you have no reason to be confident. Let me help you create new confidence. Let me help you rebuild your belief in you.

Step 1: Be courageous.

Believing in yourself is the foundation of your success. But what do you do when you don't believe in you? What do you do when your confidence is shot, or you feel you have no *reason* to be confident? The answer is to lean into courage. Courage builds confidence.

Award-winning author and speaker Mel Robbins says, "Confidence in yourself is built through everyday acts of courage." In other words, the precursor to confidence is courage. And courage is nothing more than taking everyday action—no matter how scared, nervous, intimidated, or unsure you are.

If you were to visit my home in St. George, Utah, you'd see a detailed mural of a majestic, golden-brown lion watching over, even guarding, our indoor basketball court. That lion is an ode to Mark Batterson's bestselling book *Chase the Lion*. The theme of the book encourages people to go against "normal" and run toward the "roar," not away from it.

Courage is
nothing more
than taking
everyday action—
no matter how
scared, nervous,
intimidated, or
unsure you are.

Picture your dream or your vision as a five-hundred-pound lion with three-inch fangs roaring directly at you. Most people ignore the "roar" of their dreams, or worse, they run from it. That roaring lion scares them. It drowns out their confidence. Yet all they need is a little courage to begin chasing that lion.

My point is, you can have courage—even if you don't have confidence. And you build confidence by being courageous.

"Be the one" who has the courage to run toward the roar.

Step 2: Shift your attitude.

The founding father of the historical novel, Sir Walter Scott, once said, "For success, attitude is equally as important as ability." And nearly every world-class athlete, coach, author, scientist, entrepreneur, and leader—from Venus Williams to Winston Churchill—have sung the praises of having the right attitude.

The single best thing about attitude is that you don't need any external force to shift or change it. Your attitude is not dependent on any person or event. You don't have to sell, prospect, or persuade. You're in total control.

So, let me ask you some questions: What's one attitude shift you can make right now that will move you closer to your vision?

Can you show up with better energy? Can you be a better listener? Can you set the "temperature" of the room? Can you radiate positivity? Can you exercise more patience? Can you be more empathetic? Can you avoid whining, complaining, or blaming?

I want you to pinpoint one attitude shift you can make right now that will guide you closer to your vision. Then make that shift.

Remember, you don't need permission to shift your attitude.

Step 3: Take physical action.

The bestselling author of *How to Win Friends and Influence People*, Dale Carnegie, says, "Inaction breeds doubt and fear. Action breeds confidence and courage." With that in mind, what's the next physical action step you can take right now that will move you closer to your vision? Is it replying to the email that's been clogging your inbox? Is it making that call you've been putting off? Is it having that difficult conversation you've been avoiding?

Can I tell you something that seems so obvious but something we often miss?

The world's tallest mountains are climbed one step at a time. The world's greatest books are written one page at a time. The world's biggest empires are built one brick at a time. All you need to do is take that first physical step forward. That alone will give you confidence. In fact, it will give you confidence to take the next step forward. Then the next. Then the next. And the next.

Every step you take creates new confidence because every step moves you closer to your vision. Suddenly, your dreams won't seem so far away. So impossible. So out of reach. Simply because you'll be physically moving toward them. And, with that, you'll be breeding new confidence.

So, take that next step today. Take that next step now.

THE SECOND C: COMMITMENT

Get Committed; Stay Committed

I can't recall exactly where I first heard it, but I remember motivational speaker Zig Ziglar once saying something like, "Most people have the commitment level of a kamikaze pilot on their forty-seventh mission." Think about it this way: Have you ever listened to a podcast, watched a video, or attended an event that lit you up? Something that sparked a fire in your soul. And just like that you were all in. Totally committed.

"I got this!"

Then something happened, right? Maybe a client left you hanging. A naysayer got you down. You had a bad day. And next thing you know, you're out.

"Screw it."

Then what happened? You read a powerful book. Received an exciting email. Had a great conversation.

Something lifted your spirits and reignited your fire. And bam! You're in again.

"I'm back, baby!"

And then what? The cycle repeated itself, didn't it? Another down day. Another unfortunate event. Another reason to be out.

"C'ya."

You're in. You're out. You're out. You're in. It's as unsettling as riding a 500-foot roller coaster constructed entirely of drops and twists and turns and loops.

Now, let me ask you: In math, what's the fastest way to go from point A to point B?

It's a straight line.

So what if you had a "straight-line" commitment? In other words, what if you get committed and *stay* committed . . . on the good days and on the bad days?

Life isn't linear. There are ups and downs. But to "be the one," you must get and stay committed. You must maintain what I call your "straight-line" commitment.

In fact, research suggests that 92 percent of people don't stick to their commitments.[12] If you want to be in the top 8 percent, go all in. Maintain your straight-line commitment. Because there are no lukewarm winners in life.

The following three steps or mantras will help you get committed and stay committed.

Step 1: Trust the process.

The following is a tried-and-true process that every real-life success story follows:

1. Dream
2. Struggle
3. Victory

But here's the key to victory that most people miss: Each step of this process is the same size. You see, most people want a big dream, a small struggle, and a big victory. As you know, that's just not how it works. You can't achieve a "Ten" dream with a "Three" commitment. You won't survive the struggle. You'll give up long before you experience victory.

You have a big dream to "be the one," which means you've signed yourself up for a struggle that's equal to or commensurate with your dream. So, when you're in that struggle, remember it's part of the process. And the next step is a victory.

A victory equal to the size of your struggle.

So, when your commitment is put to the test, trust the process. Stay the course through the struggle. And know that you're paying the price for a bigger victory.

Because the bigger the struggle, the better the story. The bigger the struggle, the louder the applause. And the bigger the struggle, the bigger the victory.

Trust the process and stay committed.

The bigger the struggle, the better the story. The bigger the struggle, the louder the applause. And the bigger the struggle, the bigger the victory.

Step 2: Never quit on a bad day.

I know plenty of people who would tell you, "Never quit." I don't believe in that. Maybe there are some things you should quit. Imagine if Steve Jobs never quit Atari. Imagine if Barbara Corcoran never quit her job as a waitress. Imagine if Tony Robbins never quit his gig as a janitor.

It's not that you should never quit. It's that you should never quit on a bad day.

When's the last time you had a bad day? Last month? Last week? Today?

Remember, the darkest hour is the one right before dawn. Therefore, new beginnings and break-throughs are always near. Just as the day resets when the sun begins to rise, allow yourself to "reset" after dark days so you don't quit seconds before your biggest breakthrough.

Make the commitment to never quit on a bad day.

Step 3: Persist until you succeed.

The word "until" won't just make your success possible. Nor probable. It will make your success *inevitable*. It will *guarantee* your success.

The late Augustine "Og" Mandino devoted one of the affirmations from his book *The Ten Ancient Scrolls for Success* to this concept. It reads, "I will persist *until* I succeed."[13]

You see, most people persist until things get hard. Until someone says no. Until a tough day, week, month, or year. The bottom line is, they persist until they quit.

Is that you? Do you persist until you quit or a client leaves or a customer throws a fit or a family member makes you feel less than or a hater pushes your hot buttons or . . . or . . . or . . . ?

Professional boxer "Iron" Mike Tyson famously said, "Everyone has a plan, until they get punched in the face." Are you only going to persist until you get "punched in the face"?

Or are you going to "be the one" by persisting until you succeed?

There will almost certainly be times when you need to update the word that comes before *until*. You may need to *change* until you succeed, *grow* until you succeed, or *adapt* until you succeed. But *until* will always be there. It is the word that remains untouched. It is the word guaranteeing your success.

Persist *until* you succeed.

THE THIRD C: COMPETENCE

Create Competence

"Don't leave," lit up on my phone. I was across the country in Florida when I read that text from my brother. "I'm going to fly out for the game."

It was fall, and we had the rare opportunity to see our beloved University of Utah Utes take on the Florida Gators in football at Ben Hill Griffin Stadium, also known as "The Swamp." We had the even rarer opportunity to sit in the front row—at the 50-yard line!—of the legendary stadium. During the game, it almost felt like we were on the field. We observed everything in great detail. And yet the one thing that stood out to me most, the one thing I couldn't miss, was the iconic Michael Jordan "Jumpman" logo . . . everywhere. That timeless silhouette of the world's greatest basketball player was visible on every UF player from head to toe; it adorned their helmets and their jerseys and their pants and their socks and their cleats. It marked every piece of equipment on the sidelines. Even the coaches and the trainers and the water coolers were united by the "Jumpman."

The crazy thing is, Michael Jordan played basketball, not football.

And his claim to fame was his professional career, not his collegiate.

Plus he'd already been retired for twenty years.

Yet he was everywhere for one reason: he built skill above his talent.

Talent refers to your innate gifts or abilities. The things you were born with. The raw material you've been given.

Talent comes naturally. Skill, on the other hand, is acquired.

That means skills can be learned, taught, and duplicated. They're earned, not given. And you have the opportunity and ability to learn and develop skills that can take you far beyond what your talent can do alone. In other words, you can build skill above your talent.

Michael Jordan was the greatest player in basketball history. He's a six-time NBA champion, two-time Olympic gold medalist, and five-time NBA MVP. He received the Presidential Medal of Freedom from the forty-fourth president of the United States, Barack Obama, and he's been inducted into the basketball hall of fame . . . *twice.* But have you ever watched Michael Jordan play?

He had talent, no doubt. But that's not what made him the greatest basketball player ever.

He was fast, but not the fastest. He was strong, but not the strongest. He was tall, but not the tallest. In fact, he was just six-foot-six. Michael Jordan was the fourth *shortest* player on the Chicago Bulls '97–'98 championship roster.

If you assessed him by his talent alone, from his speed to his height, few, if any, would have pegged him to be the greatest ever. That's why, to many, including some of his own coaches, Michael Jordan's rise to super-stardom was somewhat of a surprise.

So what made MJ the greatest ever?

He was obsessed, meticulous, and even maniacal about developing his skills. In fact, it visibly bugs him when people credit his talent instead of his skills for his success. A stirring, nationwide, Nike television commercial, dubbed "Maybe It's My Fault," aired during MJ's heyday to clear things up.

As a montage of Jordan's greatest moments light up the screen, his deep, distinctive voice is heard narrating: "Maybe I led you to believe it was easy, when it wasn't. Maybe I led you to believe my game was built on flash and not fire. Maybe I led you to believe that basketball was a God-given gift and not something I worked for every single day of my life."

His point was simple: His success wasn't given, it was earned. It was earned by building skill above his talent.

In a candid conversation with Jordan's college bas-ketball teammate and Emmy-winning analyst, Kenny "the Jet" Smith, Smith adamantly reinforced this: "Jordan's stuff is not an accident. It's not like, oh he was gifted . . . no! He was the most fundamentally sound player that ever played the game. His left hand is in the correct passing lane. His footwork is impeccable. His jump shot was pure. His feet stay still."[14]

Talent is your floor. Skill is your ceiling.

Do you see what Smith intentionally focused on? It was not Michael Jordan's talent. He focused only on his skill.

As MJ himself put it, "Take everything you've been given and make something better." In other words, build skill above your talent.

So, here's my question to you: Are you relying on talent, or are you intentionally building skill above your talent?

Talent is your floor. Skill is your ceiling.

Let me show you how to build skill above your talent to create competence.

Step 1: Schedule time for skill development.

Success will not attack you.

Think about that. Most people leave their skill development to hope. They hope they get better over time. Or they hope they have time to get to it. They hope the skills attack them.

What about you?

When's the last time you made time for skill development? Did you finish that book? Did you record that podcast? Did you attend that training?

The problem is simple: we rarely schedule time to develop our skills. Sure, we may buy or invest in the resources. The book. The podcast. The training. But then they just get tacked on to our to-do list like everything else.

And then what happens?

They slide down (and eventually off) that list, as other to-dos take priority, and your time, motivation, and focus slowly slip away.

The crazy thing is, you schedule time to watch the game, don't you? You schedule time to catch the movie or the show. You schedule time for wine night or happy hour. You schedule time for vacation. And you schedule time for the concert.

So why don't you schedule time to develop your skills? Why don't you schedule time to raise your "ceiling"?

You'll find the vast majority of successful people schedule time to develop their skills. Warren Buffett does. Sara Blakely does. Mark Cuban does.

How about you?

Use that time you schedule to develop two types of skills: soft skills and hard skills. Soft skills are interpersonal; they can be things like your communication, your teamwork, your leadership, your energy, your empathy, or your attitude. Hard skills, on the other hand, are technical; they can be things like marketing, presenting, writing, sales, negotiation, and follow-up. Just like a world-class doctor needs empathy and expertise, an elite architect needs to be creative while designing to code, and a successful attorney needs to be both knowledgeable and persuasive, you need to be competent in both categories to "be the one."

If someone were to ask you *when* you're developing your skills, make sure you have an answer. And tell them what you're working on. Don't just put skill development on your to-do list. Schedule untouchable time for it.

Go block it off; schedule time for skill development right now.

Step 2: Seek feedback.

To develop competence and skill, you must seek feedback. There is a Japanese concept called *shoshin*, which translates to "the beginner's mind."

In martial arts, it refers to maintaining a "white-belt mentality" as you climb the ranks. In fact, your first black belt is derived from the same word. It's called *shodan*, translated as "first level."

Do you see the connection?

Shoshin is a wise reminder to never think, or assume, that you've arrived—no matter how far you've come. It's also a wise reminder to intentionally seek feedback like any beginner would.

As I say to the people on my teams and in my organizations, leaders run to the information. They do not wait for the information to find them. They sprint toward others to seek honest feedback.

Who are you running to? Who are you sprinting to? Who are you seeking feedback from? Don't avoid feedback. Embrace it. Put any ego aside and ask questions: How can I learn? How can I improve? What could I have done better? It may be uncomfortable. It may make you anxious or insecure. But that "white-belt mentality" will take you from good to great.

Build skill and create competence by seeking feedback from people around you.

Step 3: Prepare with excellence.

There may be no better example of the power of preparation than the story of Winston Churchill. The man whose words changed the course of history and earned him a Nobel Prize had little natural talent. In fact, he had a shocking hindrance.

This iconic orator had a speech impediment. An impediment he overcame with preparation and skill. Famously, Churchill spent one *hour* in preparation for every *minute* he spoke! That's why many have called the secret of his success "immense preparation."

But Churchill wasn't the only great "one" to promote the power of preparation. Bobby Knight, one of the winningest college basketball coaches of all time (who also coached Michael Jordan in the Olympics), has been quoting as saying, "The key is not the will to win.

Everybody has that. It is the will to prepare to win that is important."

What are you doing to prepare to win? How are you preparing with excellence? You can't wing it and still win. Never assume; always anticipate. Churchill didn't assume. He anticipated. That way, nothing is left to chance.

Create competence by preparing with excellence.

"Be the one" who is confident, committed, and competent.

CHAPTER
6

Elevate Your Emotional Maturity

I vividly remember the day I decided to be an entrepreneur. To start my first business. To cut off all other possibilities. To stop saying "tomorrow" and to dedicate myself to my dream. I declared it to my wife on a Sunday morning: "Honey, I'm going to do this! We're going to do this!"

I was twenty-five years old and already a family man: father to a tender one-year-old boy, Isaac, and husband to the love of my life, Missy.

With no college education under my belt, I had been selling animated Bible videos from a mall kiosk to support my family; building my own business and being an entrepreneur would be quite different from what I was used to. But I'd made up my mind.

Later that morning, we went to church. After the congregational meeting, I was waiting in the hallway for Sunday school to start, when I bumped into two of my church "friends."

You probably have "friends" like these. They aren't necessarily your real friends, but you catch up when you cross paths. At the gym. On social media. Around the office. Or in my case, at church. With these kinds of friends, your relationship rarely goes deeper than surface-level, and your conversations rarely exceed small talk.

Which is exactly what occurred in the church hallway.

"How was your week?" I asked.

One "friend" gave the equivalent of "meh."

"And you?" I asked the other.

Same answer.

Both were unhappy at their jobs. Unhappy with their lives. Unhappy in general.

Manning that mall kiosk certainly wasn't my dream job. But unlike them, I wasn't unhappy. I had Isaac. I had Missy. And as of that morning, I had a business to build.

So, when the conversation turned to me, I decided to tell my "friends" about the decision I had made that very morning. I knew what I was about to share transcended small talk, but I hoped their support and faith in me would make any lingering self-doubt dissipate.

"I'm starting a business," I said. "I just committed this morning."

The second those words left my mouth, laughter filled the hallway. My "friends'" laughter.

There were no "Congratulations!" No pats on the back. Not even a single word of encouragement. In fact, it was just the opposite. My dream was comical to them. I was the butt of their jokes. My decision and declaration, the punch line.

And they didn't stop there. They began to make fun of me, talking to each other as if I wasn't standing right in front of them. "Are you kidding me? This guy?"

Then they talked directly to me. "What are you going to do, Justin? Fire your boss?" "Let me guess—you're gonna become a millionaire, right?" "What a joke. Good luck, buddy!"

Just like that, these two downers were happy as clams—at my expense. I felt mocked. Criticized. Ridiculed. Shamed. And embarrassed.

They made me feel stupid for dreaming bigger than that little mall kiosk.

Have you ever had something like this happen to you? You share something important, a goal, dream, or decision, and instead of encouraging you, people make fun of you? Maybe they mock, criticize, ridicule you, or shame you?

Before I share how I responded to my so-called friends making fun of me, can we agree that this is a judgment-free zone? I won't judge you, and you won't judge me in how I handled things. Remember, I was young.

At that moment, I experienced three distinct emotions. The first was anger—I mean, I wanted to knock these two dudes out! I was in shock. I wasn't a little kid anymore. I wasn't even a teenager. I was a man, with a family! And two other men were making fun of me. To my face . . . at church!

If you're going to make fun of me, at least do it behind my back.

You know what's even crazier? My "friends" didn't know that I was a former Junior Olympics boxer. I was literally trained to fight. For a split second—and only in my mind—that church hallway transformed into a boxing ring. I pictured myself throwing two lightning-fast left hooks. Chin, chin. Just like I'd drilled thousands of times before.

Fortunately, my mind was moving far faster than my actions. I pictured our bishop walking by, stepping over the two men out cold on the floor, then turning to the bystanders with wide, frightened eyes and asking aloud, "What happened here?"

"Those two were making fun of brother Justin's dreams. And the next thing we knew . . ."

Then, *poof*, I had snapped out of it, back to reality, and back to the hallway, not the imaginary boxing ring.

As my shock subsided, I was hit with my second emotion: I wanted to verbally defend myself.

I felt like I needed to defend myself. I wanted to defend my decision to chase my dreams. I wanted to look these guys in the eye and say: *You guys hate your lives! At least I'm trying to succeed. I might fail. But at least I'm going for it!*

Then the third emotion hit me: regret. I actually regretted telling them about my decision to start a business. I had shared something with these guys that was personal, thinking I could trust them. Thinking they might help.

I was wishing I could rewind time. I saw myself snatching my own words out of thin air as they left my lips, and shoving them back into my mouth before they ever reached my "friends."

But it wasn't just regret over sharing my decision with them. I was tempted to regret even dreaming in the first place. If I could take back those words, it'd be as if it never happened. No harm, no foul. What a relief! Forget my big dreams. I could go right back to playing small.

You see, no one made fun of me when they saw me at the mall, because no one makes fun of you when you live under your potential. No one mocks you. Criticizes you. Ridicules you. Or shames you. They have no reason to. Because nobody cares when you play small.

So, that was Day One of pursuing my dreams.

But here's the thing: Something similar happens to everybody who dreams big. To people who go for their potential, who put it all on the line.

It will happen to you. It will happen to you as you commit to "be the one."

It might not be on day one. It may be week one. Month one. Even year one. But it will happen. Because people will doubt you when you stop playing small and start dreaming big.

You see, I've had the privilege of traveling around the world. I've spoken on stages in thirty-plus countries. And in every country and every culture, the dreamer, "the one," experiences this kind of thing.

In Asia, they say the nail that sticks up shall be hammered down. In other words, if you have big dreams, you will be pounded down like a nail.

They hammer "the one" down with sayings like: Conform. Stand down. Duck your head.

In Australia, New Zealand, and throughout the UK, they have a name for this social norm. It's called the "tall poppy syndrome." The tallest poppy, or flower, is always cut down.

People will
doubt you
when you
stop playing
small and start
dreaming big.

How dare somebody stick up? It's as if dreaming big is a criminal act.

And we have our own version of this here in the US. Are you familiar with the "crab mentality"? If you put one crab in a bucket, it can crawl right out. But what happens when you put two crabs in a bucket? When one tries to crawl out, the other pulls it down.

The attitude is if I can't have it, neither can you.

"The one" is hammered in one country, cut down in another, and pulled down in a third. My friend, there are going to be people who hammer you, cut you, and pull you down on your pursuit to "be the one." You must be prepared for it.

Maybe your spouse unintentionally instills doubt in you. Maybe a parent openly questions your decisions. Maybe a sibling lashes out at you with jealousy. Maybe total strangers make nasty comments. Maybe a customer goes crazy on you. Maybe friends get envious. Maybe other "friends" crack jokes at your expense.

I know how much that hurts. I understand that feeling. So, how do you handle it? How do you respond? How do you move forward?

The answer is simple: elevate your emotional maturity.

UCLA's iconic men's basketball coach, John Wooden, said: "All of life is peaks and valleys. Don't let the peaks get too high and the valleys too low."

Coach Wooden went so far as to train his players on emotional maturity. When reporters entered the locker room after a big game, they could never tell if the team won or lost, because the players didn't get too high, or too low. This was intentional. Wooden's athletes were emotionally mature. And they were victorious. They were champions. He was a champion.

Emotional maturity is your response to adversity. It's how you handle peaks, and more importantly, valleys. So let me show you how to elevate your emotional maturity.

Step 1: Own your R.

The following is a simple formula to both measure and elevate your emotional maturity in any situation: $E + R = O$.

E stands for event. R stands for response. O stands for outcome. Therefore, Event + Response = Outcome.

There are three key takeaways to pull from this formula: The first is that E does not equal O. The *events* of your life do not equal the *outcomes* of your life.

You can't always control the events in your life. As you know, things happen. And you can't always control the outcomes either. However those events don't create the outcomes themselves.

You can always control your *response* to those events because your R is part of the equation. In fact, it actually

influences the outcomes. It's the only part of the equation you have total control over.

Don't be a victim to the events of your life. Be a vic-
tor to your *response* to your events. Own your *R*.

The second takeaway is that the *R* does not stand for
reaction. The *R* stands for *response*.

What happens when events or things happen to
you? What happens when stuff hits the fan? Do you
react or respond?

The great martial artist, actor, and philosopher,
Bruce Lee, perfectly described the difference between
the two. He called it a "mind like water." Picture a completely still pond. Nobody around. No ripples in the
water. Nothing to disrupt it.

If you were to toss a rock into that still pond, what
would happen? Imagine the splash. The ripples. The
bubbles. Even the sound. How does the water react?

Lee would say that it doesn't react. It *responds*. And
the water's response is equal to the size and velocity of
the rock. In other words, the water responds appropriately to the rock.

Now, imagine the events of your life as rocks, and
you are a still pond. Are your responses appropriate to
the size and velocity of the rocks that are tossed your
way? Is your mind like water?

Don't react to the events of your life. Press pause. Take a beat and a breath. Then respond appropriately. Respond, don't react.

The third and final takeaway is that your *R* creates an *E* for others. Said differently, the way you choose to respond to events creates events for other people.

What events are you creating for the people in your life? What events are you creating for your kids? What events are you creating for your spouse? What events are you creating for your customers, your clients, or your colleagues?

Your *R* doesn't just shape the outcome of *your* life, it creates events in *their* lives. So own your *R*. Respond, don't react. And create positive events for others.

Step 2: Be resilient.

The definition of *resilience* is to "withstand or recover quickly from difficult situations." That's why "the one" asks two key questions when adversity hits: How far do I fall? And how long do I stay down?

Almost all of us have met someone who has been through some intense adversities and got stuck at rock bottom. Say they experienced divorce. Bankruptcy. Addiction. Or the like. They went all the way down. And they're still there. Stuck.

But have you ever met someone who had faced a similar situation, similar adversities, but has done the opposite? This person hit rock bottom, yet bounced back, and is now living an unforgettable life?

There could be just one key difference between the two: emotional maturity. Emotionally mature people are resilient.

As you face your next challenge, ask yourself those two key questions: How far do I fall? And how long do I stay down?

Fall lightly. And bounce back up. Be resilient.

Step 3: Convert the hurt.

You've chosen to own your *R*. To respond appropriately. To create positive events for others. To be resilient. But that doesn't mean you won't feel pain.

When others hammer, cut, and pull you down, it hurts. I don't suggest you attempt to hide or mask that pain. Nor should you act as if you don't care or that it doesn't faze you.

Instead, I suggest that you feel that pain. Let it hurt. But then "convert the hurt" from pain to fuel.

Picture a solar panel. A solar panel converts the sun's rays into energy. It takes the pounding. It absorbs the heat. And then it turns that heat into energy. And you can—and should—do the same. Use that hurt, that

I suggest that you feel that pain. Let it hurt. But then "convert the hurt" from pain to fuel.

pain, those proverbial "rocks" hurled at you, to fuel your success.

Let your pain fuel your faith. Let your pain fuel your dreams. Let your pain propel you forward, instead of forcing you down. That's what emotionally mature people do. That's what "the one" does.

Own your R, be resilient, and convert the hurt.

"Be the one" who is emotionally mature.

7

Amplify Your Associations

What if I told you that the most powerful words in American history were almost left unsaid? And that you don't know the real truth behind one of the most pivotal moments of the past, a moment that we still honor today.

You see, hours before Dr. Martin Luther King Jr.'s unforgettable words, "I have a dream," echoed across a sea of more than 250,000 supporters in the heart of Washington, DC, Dr. King met with his advisors to fine-tune his script. But when Dr. King suggested sharing his "dream" on the biggest platform he'd ever seen, his advisors said no. Absolutely not, Martin.

It was virtually unanimous. They called his "dream" overused. Trite. Even cliché.

A passionate preacher, Dr. King had already spoken of his "dream" in every church house, on every street corner, and from every makeshift stage he'd been granted access to. That's why his advisors felt the audience needed to hear something new. Something bigger. Something better.

After all, the exposure would be dramatic. This wasn't a church house, street corner, or makeshift stage. This was *the* Lincoln Memorial, a towering tribute to one of America's greatest presidents and a gleaming symbol of hope, freedom, and unity. This was the stage where Dr. King could finally change the world. And apparently his "dream" wasn't powerful enough to do that.

That's why Dr. King's "dream" was left off the final script. In fact, it was removed hours before his speech. And when Dr. King took that stage in front of the Lincoln Memorial, guess what he did?

He stuck to the script.

He spoke of a "bad check" America tried to cash, instead of his "dream." And as expected, coming from the iconic orator, it was still a stirring and powerful speech. But it felt like something was missing. Yet Dr. King didn't deviate from the script. He spoke for nearly eleven straight minutes, his full allotted time. And the word *dream* wasn't used once.

That is, until he heard a familiar voice echo above the crowd from the steps behind him. The voice of a friend, gospel singer Mahalia Jackson, who cried out: "Tell them about the dream, Martin! Tell them about the dream!"

When Dr. King heard his friend's voice, he slid his prepared speech away, gripped the lectern with both hands, and looked out at the faces of the hundreds of thousands of people gathered in front of him. It was his largest audience ever. His life mission was at stake. And after fully absorbing the moment, he heeded Mahalia Jackson's urgings. He deviated from the script. He spoke slowly, deliberately, as only he could . . .

"So even though we face the difficulties of today and tomorrow, I still have a dream." Those words rang out across the crowd. "I have a dream that my four little children will one day live in a nation where they will not be judged by the color of their skin, but by the content of their character.

"I have a dream today. That little black boys and little black girls will be able to join hands with little white boys and little white girls as sisters and brothers. I have a dream today."

The rest is history. Dr. King's "I Have a Dream" speech was his most powerful. His most moving. His most impactful. Yet without Mahalia Jackson, those unforgettable words would have been left unsaid. Imagine that . . .

So I want to ask you: Who are you listening to? Who do you associate with? Who is *your* Mahalia?

Let me give you my take on some common advice. You've heard the idea that you're the average of the five people you spend the most time with. And yes, I believe there's some truth to that. But if you ask me, it's an incomplete concept.

Can you really surround yourself with five people you aspire to be like? Can you do this 24/7, 365? In reality, it seems almost impossible, doesn't it? But even if you could surround yourself with five greats, what if I told you you'd be doing yourself a disservice? What if I told you that you'd be missing out by *not* surrounding yourself with other people?

I believe that's exactly what would happen. That's why I'd like to guide you through a more complete strategy to help you amplify your associations. Admittedly, it's a strategy you've probably never heard of. But it's also a strategy that can change your world. I call it the "Rule of 33." And not only is it simple, it's also practical. You can apply it today and benefit by tomorrow.

Instead of chasing the impossible by spending nearly all of your time with five people you aspire to be like, distribute your time equally among three groups of associations: people ahead of you, people where you are, and people behind you.

It's called the "Rule of 33" because your time is split evenly among each group. Which means each of these groups get 33 percent of your time and attention.

And let me tell you why this is so powerful. Let's start from the top with the people who are ahead of you on your journey. These are the people you aspire to be like. They are people who lift you up and who will guide you to the next level.

They inspire you. They challenge you. They elevate you.

They are mentors to learn from because they've already been where you want to be. But they aren't the *only* people who matter.

So, let's talk about the next group, the people who are where you are now. What's the value in them? Well, you're on the same wavelength. Which means they are dealing with similar struggles, challenges, and obstacles.

They understand you. And you understand them. They are often your best collaborators because you are better together.

And what about the final group in your "33"? The people behind you. Are you wondering why they'd be included? How do they benefit you?

The truth is, we tend to neglect this group, don't we? We're too focused on the people ahead of us to think about the people behind us. But who you believe in is just as important as who believes in you. Who you empower is just as important as who empowers you. And who you pour into is just as important as who pours into you.

Have you ever noticed that you learn more by teaching? The people behind you give you an opportunity to mentor and to teach. You grow by giving to these associations. Pour into them to fill your cup.

Remember, even Dr. King needed Mahalia Jackson. So, I encourage you to form and complete your inner circle by applying the "Rule of 33." But don't stop there.

It's not only about who you associate with and who you listen to. Amplifying your associations is also about the weight you give their words.

A friend of mine sat next to Ronald Reagan at an awards dinner in Washington, DC, after President Reagan had left office. And my friend asked the former president a fairly basic question: "How did you become a two-term president?"

Reagan's answer was profound. He said when he was a boy, he told his friends he wanted to be a football player. Because he was small, many laughed. Some even made fun of him.

Guess what?

Reagan didn't just make his high school football team. He made his college team too. He said, "I listened to those who believed in me, and I listened to those who said I could."

Who you empower is just as important as who empowers you. And who you pour into is just as important as who pours into you.

When he was a football player, Reagan told his friends he wanted to move to Hollywood to be an actor. They thought he was crazy. Some even ridiculed him. But you probably already know that Ronald Reagan ended up in film and television and was in the industry for more than thirty years. He even starred in a football movie.

He said, "I listened to those who believed in me, and I listened to those who said I could."

When he was an actor, Reagan told his friends he wanted to be the governor of California. "With all due respect, Ron, what do you know about politics? You're an actor," they'd say. Yet he served two full terms as governor of California.

Reagan said, "I listened to those who believed in me, and I listened to those who said I could."

When he was governor of California, he told his friends he wanted to become the president of the United States. "Of course, California, of all places, would elect a celebrity as governor. But president? You? C'mon, Ron. . . ."

Ronald Reagan was elected the fortieth president of the United States. He served two terms. And he's widely considered one of the most influential presidents ever.

Now let's rewind back to my friend's original question: How?

Reagan said, "I listened to those who believed in me, and I listened to those who said I could."

Reagan said, "I listened to those who believed in me, and I listened to those who said I could."

He listened to the positive. He tuned out the negative. Which means, he tipped the scales.

Whose words are empowering you? Whose words are lifting you up? And whose words are holding you hostage or weighing you down?

Napoleon Hill studied five hundred of the most influential people in human history for his 1937 best-selling book, *Think and Grow Rich*. People like Andrew Carnegie, Henry Ford, John Rockefeller, and Thomas Edison. Of the five hundred people Hill profiled, he found that every one of them had what he referred to as "well-intentioned" friends and family who told them they'd fail.

The truth is, most of us do the opposite of King, Reagan, Carnegie, Ford, Rockefeller, Edison, and the like. Not only do we *listen* to negativity, but we allow it to *outweigh* positivity as well.

Have you ever noticed how, out of a group of dozens of positive comments on social media, one negative comment can eat away at you? How one negative person or naysayer can totally ruin an otherwise great day? How the people who say, "You can't," seem to speak louder than the people who say, "You can"? And how their words manage to mute anything, and everything, positive as they echo in your ears?

You see, we tend to put more weight into the words of those who laugh at, who make fun of, who ridicule, who doubt, and who question us, than those who, as Reagan put it, "tell us that we can."

Imagine if Dr. King allowed his advisors' words to outweigh Mahalia Jackson's. Imagine if Ronald Reagan gave more weight to the words of the people who said he "can't." Imagine if Carnegie, Ford, Rockefeller, or Edison favored the words of their "well-intentioned" friends and family.

For many of us, negativity weighs tons. And positivity weighs ounces. But not if you're striving to "be the one." Amplify your associations by applying the "Rule of 33." Then tip the scales by listening more to the positive than the negative.

The power of associations isn't just backed by these stories. It's also backed by science. It can be seen in an incredible study on obesity shared in the *New England Journal of Medicine.* The study revealed the astonishing results of a thirty-year analysis on a social network of more than twelve thousand people. Researchers found that if just one person in that social network became obese, those closely connected to them had a greater chance of becoming obese too. According to the study, if a person you consider a friend becomes obese, your own chances of becoming obese skyrocket 57 percent. In fact, even thin individuals were more likely to gain weight if just *one* of their associations gained weight.[15]

In other words, all it took was one person in a massive circle of associations to "spread" or "transfer disease." But that's not all. Researchers also found that the influence of associations transcends proximity. For example, there was no effect among neighbors, unless they were also friends. But obesity was able to spread from one friend to another, even when they were miles, states, and even countries apart. "It's not that obese or non-obese people simply find other similar people to hang out with," warned study co-author Nicholas Christakis of Harvard Medical School. "Rather, there is a direct, causal relationship."[16] As the *New York Times* put it, obesity was "contagious" among friends.[17]

Think about that . . .

Your associations, near and far, affect everything from your health and happiness to your behavior and beliefs. If a complex disease as extreme as obesity is socially contagious, and is capable of spreading from person to person, so can negativity that derails your confidence, commitment, competence, and more.

So, who's in your "33"? Who do you need to add? Who do you need to remove? Who are you collaborating with? Who are you pouring into? Who's pouring into you? Who do you need to listen to less? Who do you need to listen to more? Who's your Mahalia?

Use the following lines to brainstorm a list of people in your life that belong in your "33." Then think about each person and assess (and label) if they are ahead (*a*) of you, at the same (*s*) level, or behind (*b*) you. Add and edit as needed to ensure each of your "33" has an equal number of positive people.

_____

_____

_____

_____

_____

_____

_____

Apply the "Rule of 33." Surround yourself with people ahead of you, behind you, and where you are now. Listen to those who believe in you and say you can.

"Be the one" who amplifies their associations.

CHAPTER

8

Speak Life into Your Future

Renowned sports psychologist and the man *Sports Illustrated* dubbed "the world's best brain trainer," the late Trevor Moawad, once shared a story he read in *Success Unlimited* magazine.[18] Moawad recounted reading that in 1973, a repairman was hired to fix a refrigerated boxcar attached to the end of a train. The crew was gone when the repairman accidentally locked himself inside the boxcar. Essentially, he was trapped inside a giant freezer. Struck with fear and panic, the man pounded and pounded on the airtight doors to no avail. There was no one around. And there was no way out.

When the crew unlocked the doors the next morning, they found the man's lifeless body lying on the floor. As they inspected the boxcar, they noticed something strange: notes scribbled on the floor beside him.

Turns out, the repairman had a pen on him. "I'm becoming colder . . ." he wrote. "Nothing to do but wait . . ." he continued. Then his final note: "These might be my last words."

They were. The repairman spent the entire night locked in a freezer that typically maintains a frigid temperature of -20°F. That's a full 52° colder than freezing. That's why the cause of death seemed so obvious: Hypothermia. He froze to death. Or so he *thought* he did . . .

After inspecting the boxcar, authorities noticed something even stranger than the notes on the floor: The freezing apparatus was broken. The temperature had held steady at a mild 55–56 degrees throughout the night. Therefore, the cool air wasn't cold enough to kill the man. The freezer was basically unplugged at the time of his death.

Well, what happened? How did he die?

It's been said that the man "thought" himself to death. The medical community calls phenomena like this "psychogenic deaths," death by "giving up."

The conclusion is that this man's thoughts killed him. But can I give you my take? It wasn't his negative thoughts alone that took his life. It was his negative *words*.

What started as thoughts became words: "These might be my last words." Those words became his destiny. Like the ancient Chinese philosopher Lao Tzu said, "Watch your thoughts, for they become your words; watch your words, for they become your actions; watch your actions, for they become your habits; watch your habits, for they become your character; watch your character, for it becomes your destiny."

The repairman's negative words weaponized his negative thoughts. His destiny was etched on the floor.

You see, as humans we're hardwired to find negativity. Our brains scan our surroundings for it. The "command center" responsible for our thoughts seeks it out like a missile. But that's not because we're negative people. It's a pure survival mechanism.

In other words, we were born that way. I'll give you an example to prove it. Think of our earliest ancestors. Go back to the days when cavemen roamed the Earth. When they rolled that giant rock back first thing in the morning, what did they do?

Admire the sunrise? Listen to the sound of water flowing nearby? Gaze at the towering mountains in the distance? Of course not. They scanned their surroundings for ominous, grey storm clouds. For fierce, saber-toothed tigers. For unfamiliar and dangerous predators and tribes. Our earliest ancestors proactively searched and scanned for anything that could

The repairman's negative words weaponized his negative thoughts. His destiny was etched on the floor.

harm or kill them. Just like we do, whether we realize it or not.

My point is, the primal part of your brain doesn't scan for the positive. It scans for the negative, because your brain's not built to make you happy. It's built to keep you alive. It's built for survival. This is why we're hardwired to find what's wrong, not what's right. We're hardwired for negativity, not positivity.

I'll give you a modern example too. Fast forward to today: Let's say you're driving down the highway. To your left, the sun begins to paint the sky in stunning reds and oranges. It's a picture-perfect sunset that you almost have to see to believe.

Do you slow down to check it out? Do you stop? Do you stare? No. At best, you give it a glance. Maybe you acknowledge it with a smile or a word or two. But you keep flying down the freeway, foot glued to the pedal, hands stuck to the wheel.

But what happens when you cruise by a car crash? Do you slow down? Do you stop? Do you stare? Yes, yes, and yes. We all do. It's because we're hardwired to seek the negative.

So, to "be the one," you must proactively rewire your brain to find the positive. But how?

I'm not suggesting you *only* think positive thoughts. That seems like a stretch, doesn't it? Could that repairman have controlled his negative thoughts? Can you control your negative thoughts? I believe you can control your thoughts only to an extent. But that's an advanced skill, which requires advanced training. And even when fully trained, negativity can still slip in.

On the other hand, you can 100 percent control the words that come out of your mouth. You're in complete control of what you say. And what you say becomes your destiny. So what words are you speaking?

What negative words do you need to cut from your vocabulary? What positive words do you need to add to your vocabulary?

After analyzing data shared by Dr. Christine Porath, a tenured professor at Georgetown University and TED speaker who studies the effects of disrespect on people, Trevor Moawad concluded that our words could be up to ten times more powerful than our thoughts. Think about that. According to Moawad, if you say a thought out loud, it could be ten times more powerful than if you only think it.

How would you like to 10x your business? Your motivation? Your happiness? Your health? Your relationships? Your success?

The secret could be to speak life into these things. To speak positivity.

But here's what's even more eye-opening. Moawad also said the same research suggests that *negativity* is actually an additional multiplier. He said negative words

Negative words can be four to seven times more powerful than positive or neutral words.

can be four to seven times more powerful than positive or neutral words. This would make negative *words* forty to seventy times more powerful than negative *thoughts*.

I believe that repairman lost his life because he spoke death to his destiny: "These might be my last words," he wrote. And they were.

I've experienced a similar phenomenon in my own life. When I was just fifteen years old, my dad set me up with a personal trainer. Picture the biggest, strongest man you know. Then slap an extra one hundred pounds of pure muscle on him, a bandana, an earring, and blankets of tattoos covering each arm. That was my trainer, D'marko.

He was six-foot-two, and over three hundred pounds of muscle. The red bandana across his forehead separated his bronze hair from his bronze body busting out of his red tank top. He was the former Mr. Utah, as well as the former Mr. Los Angeles. To this day, his picture hangs on the wall of fame at the iconic Gold's Gym in Venice Beach, California. The same Gold's Gym where Arnold Schwarzenegger was known to pump iron. In fact, in his heyday, D'marko himself probably looked a little like Arnold.

And there I was, a fifteen year old who'd never lifted a weight in my life, hiding in the back of the gym with my dad, and nervously waiting to hit the bench press for the very first time. Imagine how intimidated I was when

I realized my trainer was D'marko. The biggest guy in the gym. The behemoth walking directly toward me. As he approached me, his hand swallowed mine whole. One more shake could have ripped my arm right off of my body.

"Stand up," he said.

Yes, sir.

"Your dad wants me to train you."

Yes, sir.

"I have three rules. Number one: Never be late. It's disrespectful to you, your dad . . . and to me."

Done, I thought. The last thing I want to do is disrespect this guy. So, out of equal parts respect and terror, I committed to never breaking D'marko's first rule.

"Number two: Never show up here with rat breath. I don't want to smell your breath when I'm spotting you."

My world revolved around sports and girls at that time, so I remember thinking to myself, this is good advice! Both in and out of the gym. I'm learning from this guy already!

And then D'marko taught me a simple but significant lesson about the power of words. A lesson that truly changed my life from that day forward. (In fact, I credit this lesson for eventually helping me make the leap from selling animated Bible videos for a few bucks here and there to generating billions of dollars in revenue and consulting some of the best and brightest minds in the business world.)

"Number three: Never say you can't do something. You have a conscious and subconscious mind," he said. "And your subconscious mind will believe whatever you tell it. Even if you can't lift the weight, don't ever say you can't."

Done. You won't hear "can't" come out of my mouth, D'marko.

He was dead serious about each of his three rules, even the "rat breath." Therefore, I was dead serious about them too.

Next thing I knew, D'marko was leading me through racks of weights and rows of machines. I trailed behind, engulfed by his shadow. And once we started lifting, D'marko didn't waste any time putting his third rule to the test. He pushed me to the brink by sliding more and more weight onto each end of the stainless-steel bar after each successful rep. And with each pound added, I remember thinking to myself: *There is absolutely no way I can lift these weights. Not a chance!*

But I never said that out loud. And guess what? I could lift the weights. I was way stronger than I realized. I could accomplish way more than I realized because I never empowered my negative thoughts with words.

I followed D'marko's rule. I controlled my words. And over time, not only did I avoid saying negative words like "I can't," I proactively spoke positive words. I said, "I can."

I'd get under a barbell stacked with weights and whisper to myself, "I got this. I own this weight." And guess what? I could. I did. My positive words made me even stronger. And don't just take my word for it. Professional bodybuilder and eight-time Mr. Olympia, Ronnie Coleman, used to do the same thing. He would holler "light weight, baaabayyy" from beneath a bending barbell, seconds before successfully shattering yet another weightlifting record.

You see, you, too, have a conscious and subconscious mind. And your subconscious mind will believe whatever you tell it. That's why I believe *you* are far stronger than you may realize. Not just physically. But mentally. Emotionally. Even spiritually. And you can find that strength and create new strength with the power of the tongue.

What if you were to stop saying "I can't"? And what if you were to start saying "I can"? Your subconscious would listen. And I bet you'd amaze yourself.

I've since followed this "rule" in every aspect of my life. I've been huddled up in boardrooms of failing businesses. Flanked by stumped executives to my left and right, discussing organizations hanging on by a thread, with no solutions in sight, no reason to believe.

As a group, we would be frustrated. We were tired. We were at a loss. We didn't know what we were going to do. I didn't have the answers. At times, I had even

I controlled my words. And over time, not only did I avoid saying negative words like "I can't," I proactively spoke positive words. I said, "I can."

thought, There's no way we can do this. But guess what I *said*: "We can do this, guys. We got this. We're smart. We have good intentions. What questions are we not asking? What problems are we not solving? What is this trying to teach us?"

And sure enough, we would uncover the right answers. Now, do these words alone save businesses? Probably not. But if you ask me, they play a part in their destiny.

To this day, decades after D'marko shared his third rule with teenage me, I still never say "I can't." And my kids know not to say "I can't," either. Those words aren't allowed in our home. Not now, not ever.

Like the Bible says in Proverbs 18:21, "Death and life are in the power of the tongue."

How often do you let negativity slip out of your mouth? How often do negative thoughts transform into negative words? Speak positive, not negative. Speak life, not death.

But let me add something else: Your words aren't only about you. Your words are about others too.

Author Yehuda Berg has been quoted as saying, "Words are singularly the most powerful force available to humanity. Words have energy and power with the ability to help, to heal, to hurt, to harm, to humiliate, and to humble." In fact, a 2019 study published in the journal *Brain and Behavior* verified that negative words can actually activate the pain response in the brain.[19] For example, hearing something like "this may hurt a bit," before receiving a shot may be enough to trigger a painful response before the tip of a needle even grazes your arm.

Your words affect you. And your words affect others. So speak positive, not negative. Speak life, not death. Instead of muttering, "I'm so tired," after a long day at work, speak of the many things that you accomplished during that day. Or speak of "looking forward" to the next day. Instead of predicting a "long day," predict a "full day." Instead of saying "I have to," say, "I get to." Be more conscious of your words to speak life into your situation.

Use your words to speak life into others too. Use your words to speak life into your colleagues. Use your words to speak life into your kids. Use your words to speak life into your relationships. Remind the people who matter to you of the things that you love about them. When others think they can't, tell them they can. Instead of brushing off a compliment, give one back.

When you're locked in the proverbial freezer, don't give up. "Rewire" your words. Speak positive, not negative.

"Be the one" who speaks life into the future.

CHAPTER
9

Stack Reasons to Keep Going

Years ago, I interviewed a fascinating man named James Lawrence, a.k.a. The Iron Cowboy. James is a self-proclaimed "white Canadian dude that peaked in high school." A guy with limited genetic gifts. Limited physical abilities. And limited resources. Yet decades after high school graduation, a father well into his 30s, James began to set and shatter multiple world records in extreme endurance racing. (He's still setting records, now, in his forties.)

The crazy thing is, the man widely considered the world's toughest endurance athlete barely survived a turkey trot years earlier.

You see, his very first "race" was a Thanksgiving Day fun run with his wife back in 2005. The kind of race almost anybody can enjoy and complete, sans training, to burn a few calories hours before the day's feast and festivities.

Well, that run was anything but fun for James.

Moms pushing double-wide strollers flew by the twenty-eight year old at every mile marker. And to his bewilderment (and his wife's amusement), the not-so-fun run "destroyed" him. In other words, it left him exhausted and embarrassed. But he converted the hurt . . . and that experience pushed him to be better. In fact, that little turkey trot was the catalyst that convinced him to later train for a marathon.

The same day he completed his first marathon, he had to be carried down the stairs, then pushed across a parking lot in a wheelchair to his car. Instead of giving up, he, again, converted the hurt and found more motivation.

Next up were sprint triathlons. A stepping-stone, entry-level swim-bike-run for those aspiring to be triathletes. Then he progressed to half triathlons. Then full triathlons. And eventually he took on the toughest triathlon in the world. The Ironman. And not just one, but multiple. If you're unfamiliar with an Ironman-distance triathlon, here's the deal: it starts with a competitive 2.4-mile swim, then moves on to a bike race of 112 miles, and *ends* with a full marathon—a grueling 26.2-mile run.

Does that sound like fun? It was for James. Not only was he hooked, he was also good. He broke records.

But James wasn't satisfied. He wanted to accomplish something even tougher. He wanted to test his limits. Around that time, he heard of a man who completed fifty marathons, in fifty states, in fifty days. What could be harder than that man's 50-50-50? James's version of 50-50-50. Forget marathons. James went for fifty triathlons. Fifty *Ironman*-distance triathlons.

In 2015, James attempted his 50-50-50, where he would complete fifty full Ironman-distance triathlons, one in each of the fifty states, over fifty consecutive days. In an effort to raise money for charity, James invited the public to join him for the final five kilometers (5K) of the run portion of each race; i.e., they could finish the race with him.

His daily schedule looked like this: Swim. Bike. Run. Catch a wink or two of sleep from a cramped seat in an airplane or the confined quarters of an RV, then get up at the crack of dawn in a new state and literally dive right back into unfamiliar waters.

James got started in Hawaii. He jumped in the dark water at midnight. And after fourteen grueling hours, he completed the first of fifty Ironman-distance triathlons.

He then hopped on a flight to Alaska. The plane landed at 6:00 a.m., and he was in the water by 7:00.

Next up, Oregon. Same schedule, different day.

Three days. Three states. Three successful Ironman-distance triathlons. And . . . a grand total of six and a half hours of sleep—on commercial flights, crammed into coach, alongside screaming children.

By day four, James was ready to call it quits. His body was demanding it. Even begging for it. He had saddle sores so painful he could barely sit down, he could feel the raw, bright red blisters expanding between his toes, and sleep deprivation almost had him hallucinating.

As he hobbled toward his eldest daughter, she asked, "Dad, how are you doing?"

"I'm tired, Lucy."

"You look terrible," she said.

"Sweetheart, I feel terrible."

Lucy desperately wanted to help her daddy. She could see his pain, and she could think of only one way to offer a hand: run with him. So, with all the confidence of a naive twelve year old, she said, "Dad, I'm gonna do all of the 5Ks with you. Together we can do this! I'll be waiting. I need you to show up."

And show up he did. Running alongside Lucy became James's "why." It was his reason to keep going after four grueling days. It was an appointment he had to keep, even though it meant swimming, biking, and running a combined 140+ miles every day to be there.

That appointment with Lucy gave him a new reason to keep going. But James quickly found that one "why" wasn't enough to continue pushing himself. Not on this treacherous journey. As meaningful as his appointment with Lucy was, he needed even more reasons to keep going.

Sounds counterintuitive, doesn't it? Most of us have been taught that when we find our "why," magic will happen. Your "why" is your wand. But life's a long race. New reasons to quit appear almost every day. And as James found out, one "why" is not enough to keep going.

Just days later, James tore a muscle in his shoulder. Another reason to call it quits. Can you imagine swimming 2.4 miles, every single day . . . with one arm? And James still had forty-plus races ahead of him. Forty-plus reasons to quit.

More reasons to quit continued to pile up. Soon after tearing that muscle in his shoulder, James fell asleep on his bike. No different than falling asleep at the wheel of a car, James lost all control. He flew into the road like Superman and tumbled along the unforgiving asphalt and concrete. New sores. New cuts. New burns. New reasons to quit.

James's toenails started to rip clean off inside his blood-soaked socks. Ten more reasons to quit. They

Most of us have been taught that when we find our "why," magic will happen. Your "why" is your wand. But life's a long race.

would regrow and then rip right off again. Add another ten to the list.

A crushing concoction of cramping and hypothermia began to feel familiar and brought him to tears in the water. He was cold. Lonely. And broken. His reasons to quit continued to multiply.

To add to his physical pain, James was accused of cheating, or doping, due to his use of an IV of saline solution to recover from severe dehydration. Others accused him of charity fraud, even though the foundation he was supporting released a statement confirming they had received tens of thousands of dollars from James's efforts. Perhaps due to the hostility, some of his equipment even went "missing" at times. More and more reasons to quit.

Have you ever noticed how easy it is to find reasons to quit? We can almost manufacture them on demand. James had plenty. And so do you. Say you decide you're going to roll out of bed earlier than usual tomorrow, so you set your alarm. What might stop you from getting up and out of bed? The warm, cozy covers? The sleep in your eyes? The nearby snooze button begging you to push it for some extra shut-eye? The dark, quiet bedroom encouraging you to fall back asleep? Surely, you can think of more.

Like I said, it's easy to find reasons to quit. And new reasons arise daily.

For James, quitting was always a legitimate option. It's an option you always have too. Especially when you're trying to do something out of the ordinary.

And attempting fifty triathlons in fifty states over fifty days was certainly not ordinary. But James didn't quit. He made it to all fifty states. He made it to every appointment with Lucy. He completed all fifty Ironman-distance triathlons. And he did it in just fifty days. And it's probably no surprise that he set and shattered world records along the way.

He accomplished the impossible—even though he could have easily come up with fifty thousand reasons to quit.

What I most wanted to know from James was how he kept going. He said his appointment with Lucy wasn't enough. He needed more "whys." But this wasn't some superhuman man. This was a father of five who "peaked in high school." Wouldn't you like to know what his secret was? What kept him going when he had what seemed like every reason in the world to quit?

James referenced one simple thing: His bag full of "whys." In other words, his reasons. Not his reasons to quit, which were as clear as day. But his reasons to keep going.

Picture a drawstring bag. A bag he pulled from and added to every day. And every race. This bag of "whys" held his reasons to keep going.

He'd pluck a new reason from the bag every time he wanted to quit. And that's why the bag constantly needed to be refilled.

He found that he couldn't reuse reasons. He needed new ones. When he tore his shoulder. When he slid across the merciless concrete. When he couldn't catch a wink of sleep. When he was accused of cheating. When his toenails tore off. When the road rash spread. When the blisters ballooned. When the tears drenched his cheeks. Every time he thought he couldn't keep going, every time he wanted to quit, he plucked another reason "why" out of his bag.

That was the secret to his motivation.

Some of James's "whys" included his appointments with Lucy; there were forty. His wife, Sunny; another powerful reason to keep going. Lucy's four siblings; four more reasons. Their warm, welcoming hugs embracing him at each finish line; five more reasons. The foundation he was raising money for; the people that money could help. The donors who supported him. Even his haters became reasons to keep going.

The locals who ran alongside Lucy and him for the final five kilometers in each state also became "whys." Sometimes there were one, two, or three. Sometimes there were ten. Sometimes there were dozens, even hundreds. They'd share their stories with James, and he would use them as reasons to keep going the next day. Ten more. Dozens more. Hundreds more.

They were all "whys" waiting in his bag.

I'm sure you've been asked, "What's your why?" But have you ever been told that one "why" is not enough? James said it himself: "If I only had one 'why,' I would have quit."

So the question is, how do you find more "whys"? Let me guide you through an exercise to do just that. Let's start with three words: how, what, and why.

When searching for reasons to keep going, most of us make the mistake of asking *how*. *How* am I going to stay motivated? *How* will I do this? *How* do I keep going?

Any question that starts with how is the wrong question to ask. The real question to start with is a *what* question.

What already motivates you? *What* are your goals? *What* are you trying to accomplish?

You're here, reading this book, because you want to "be the one." So, let's say that's your goal. That's your "what."

Now here's where things get really powerful: the final word, *why*.

You stopped asking *how*. You answered *what*. Now ask yourself *why*. Specifically, why do you want to "be the one"?

Write your answer below.

_____

_____

_____

That's your first "why." One reason to keep going. Now take a look at what you just wrote down. Why is that important to you? Why does that "why" matter? Take a moment to think about that. And when you discover the answer, write it down below.

_____

_____

_____

Now you're stacking reasons. Let's keep going.

Look at the answer you just put down on the page, your second "why." Why is that important to you? Why does that "why" matter? As you discover the answer, write it down.

_____

_____

_____

You now have another reason to keep going. Your bag is expanding.

Now here's what I want you to do: I want you to stack seven total "whys." In other words, I want you to keep asking yourself, "Why is that important to me?" Then write your answer down. You've already stacked three "whys." So use the lines below to stack four more.

_____

_____

_____

_____

You see, I've guided thousands of people through this exercise. Moms, dads, entrepreneurs, executives, and more. And while their "whys" are all unique, one thing unites them: during this exercise, they feel the "magic" happen after their fourth or fifth "why." They tear up. They get emotional. New feelings emerge. That's a tell-tale sign that you've accomplished your goal of going far beyond the superficial, that you've pushed your limits, and that your reasons to keep going are moving from your head to your heart.

That is the difference maker!

As I said before, there are always reasons to quit. And there are always reasons to keep going. It's the

Your reasons to keep going must outnumber *and* outweigh your reasons to quit.

reasons you choose that will define you. The key is this: Your reasons to keep going must outnumber *and* outweigh your reasons to quit. Your "whys" must outnumber your "why-nots" and outweigh them too.

In other words, your reasons to keep going must have breadth and depth.

The "whys" you find when you go four, five, six, and even seven layers deep—the ones in your heart, not just your head—are the ones that carry the most weight. Those are the "whys" that weigh tons, not ounces.

So the next time you're ready to quit, don't ask yourself *how*. Ask yourself *what*. Then ask yourself *why*.

"Why is that important to you?"

Now before we move on, let's revisit James. After accomplishing his near-impossible 50-50-50, James came up with a new challenge he called "Conquer 100." One hundred Ironman-distance triathlons in one hundred consecutive days.

And guess what? He did it.

He had found new reasons to keep going. He had more "whys."

You see, your "whys" will change and grow as new obstacles appear and new challenges and goals arise. Old "whys" won't carry the weight they used to. You will need to stack new and heavier reasons to keep going. That's another reason why you need to do this exercise.

That's why you need to go seven "whys" deep. That's why you need to fill your bag.

After James completed the Conquer 100, he decided he wasn't done. On day 101, he did one more—another Ironman-distance triathlon.

There are always reasons to quit. There are always reasons to keep going. And there are always reasons to do one more.

"Be the one" who stacks reasons to keep going.

CHAPTER

10

Magnify Your Focus

How often do you feel stressed out? Overwhelmed? Anxious? Or even frantic? Does your to-do list consume you? Do you ever feel like you work too hard but accomplish too little?

These are all symptoms of the same problem. Distraction.

Distraction is an epidemic, an addiction, and a disorder, all rolled into one. It's been linked to obesity, insomnia, anxiety, depression, and more . . . in kids and adults.[20] And data suggests up to 98 percent of us are regularly distracted. I've seen Harvard clinical psychologist John Ratey quoted as saying, "Compulsive use of mobile phones and computers and tablets is an addiction similar to sex, drugs, and alcohol." In fact, phone addiction is more common than sex addiction, drug addiction, and alcoholism *combined*, with nearly half of Americans admitting they are "addicted" to their cell phones.[21]

Did you know that everyday distractions like a single email, tweet, or Facebook comment can trigger the release of the brain's "feel-good" chemical, dopamine? Guess what else releases dopamine—cocaine. So it's no wonder there are now therapeutic programs in psychiatric hospitals across the US dedicated to treating social media addiction, among other distraction-related dangers.

Distraction is a drug. The "pull" of it is that strong.

A study from the University of London revealed that when you multitask, you operate at the same cognitive function as if you stayed up all night. The same research suggests that multi-tasking doesn't just slow you down—it lowers your IQ.[22] Your brain can't multitask, but distraction encourages us to keep trying.

Distraction causes stress. It causes anxiety. It even causes injury. Emergency room data in the United States shows that injuries to the neck, face, eyes, nose, and head have risen "steeply" over the last twenty years, attributing tens of thousands of ER visits to distracted driving, walking, and texting.[23] A clear description of "multitasking." If that's not scary enough, cell phone distraction-related deaths (yes, *deaths*) are on the rise as well. The

National Safety Council found 2,841 people died in distraction-affected crashes in 2018. And the Governors Highway Safety Association estimated there were more than 6,000 pedestrian deaths in 2018 alone . . . the highest number in more than twenty years.[24] Unless something changes, those numbers will surely rise in the coming months, years, and decades as new and stronger distractions emerge.

Plus, distraction steals our most valuable asset, time, in bunches. The average person spends nearly 78,000 hours of their life watching television. That's about nine full years wasted in front of the TV. Nearly a full decade of your life, gone. And here's the kicker: that doesn't account for the nearly 3,000 hours of your life spent just deciding, or debating, what to watch.[25]

Distraction snatches money out of our pockets too. Jonathan Spira, author of *Overload! How Too Much Information Is Hazardous to Your Organization*, estimates distractions cost the US economy almost one *trillion* dollars per year.[26] (In just a second, I'll show you how to calculate how much distraction is costing you.)

Like I said, 98 percent of people today are distracted. They're consumers—not creators.

That's why I want to help you cure your distraction problem. Can I show you the single best remedy? If you follow along and apply what I share, this simple cure will help you sprint circles around the sleepwalkers.

The solution
to distraction
is focus. Said
differently,
focus is your
superpower.

You see, the solution to distraction is focus. Said differently, focus is your superpower. But only 2 percent of us know how to use it.

Now, I know getting focused can feel like a familiar or expected suggestion, so let me share three things that will change the way you feel about focus . . . and encourage you to leave the life of reaction to distraction and harness your superpower.

First things first, focus magnifies effort.

The sun has the general power to heat the Earth. But do you know what happens if you focus the rays of the sun through a magnifying glass? Suddenly, those same sun rays will burn holes through pure steel. That's why inventor Alexander Graham Bell said, "The sun's rays do not burn until brought to a focus."

Imagine what would happen if you magnified your focus on the things that matter to you: your career, your health, your relationships, your family, your faith.

Your effort would magnify, and your results would multiply.

The second thing I'd like to share with you is that your focus has economic value. Focus makes you money. And distraction costs you money.

To illustrate my point, let's calculate what your focus is worth—down to the minute.

First, write down your annual income goal below. What do you want to make this year? Or what do you expect to make?

Now divide that number by 2,000 to represent the 2,000 hours the average American works each year. The result is your hourly rate, or the hourly value of your focus.

Finally, divide that number by 60 to represent the 60 minutes in each hour below. In other words, divide the hourly value of your focus from the line above by 60 to calculate your dollar-per-minute rate.

The result is your dollar-per-minute rate or what illustrious investor and "shark" Kevin Harrington calls your "dollar-per-minute analysis." That's what you're *earning* every minute you're focused. And that's what you're *burning* every minute you're distracted.

Say you want to make $125,000 this year. Your focus is worth more than $1 per minute and $60 per hour. Now think about this: The average American spends more than 1,300 hours a year on social media.[27] So what is social media—just one of many distractions—costing you? It would cost you $214 per day or $1,500 per week or more than $78,000 per year.

Want to give yourself a $78,000 raise this year? Magnify your focus.

Picture your phone as a lighter. Every time you get sucked into social media a stack of cash burns to ashes. And the same goes for all other forms of distraction.

The "father of evolution," Charles Darwin, once said, "A man who dares to waste one hour of time has not discovered the value of life." I'd say the man who dares to waste one hour of time has not discovered the value of *focus*.

And last but not least, focus is the world's strongest separator. That's its purpose. With everybody distracted, it's never been easier for you to separate yourself, to sprint around the sleepwalkers, as I said earlier. All you need to do is magnify your focus. Focus separates *your* world from *the* world. It separates the 2 percent from the 98 percent, the creators from the consumers.

And "the one" from the masses.

Now that you know its power, its value, and its purpose, let me show you my simple "5 x 5" strategy to magnify your focus:

Step 1: Clarify your top 5 strategic priorities.

Let's begin with a quick story I once heard about strategic priorities. Richard Branson, the illustrious founder of the Virgin Group, was once offered $100,000 to speak for just one hour at an event. His team rejected the offer with this response: "We're sorry, but Mr. Branson can't make it." After being declined, the offer was more than doubled. Branson and his team received a contract for $250,000 for the same one-hour speech.

"We're sorry, but Mr. Branson can't make it."

Guess what? The offer was doubled, again. Branson and his team received a contract for a whopping $500,000 for the same one-hour speech.

"We're sorry, but Mr. Branson can't make it."

Can you imagine turning down $500,000 for one hour's worth of work? The company had basically promoted Branson as its keynote speaker, so it felt obligated to get him. So that latest offer was doubled, *again.*

Branson's team received a contract for $1 million for one hour. The company even threw in a private jet to make travel easy on Mr. Branson. "Final offer," they said.

What do you think happened?

"We're sorry, but Mr. Branson can't make it."

Only this time, Branson's team provided an eye-opening explanation: "Mr. Branson is focused on his key strategic priorities. And right now speaking—for any fee—is not one of them."

Now I know what you're probably thinking. Richard Branson's filthy rich! He's one of the rare few who can afford to turn down a cool million on behalf of his "strategic priorities." And I get it. But let me ask you this question: Do you think Richard Branson got rich and then got clear on his priorities . . . or do you think he got clear on his priorities and then got rich?

What are your top five strategic priorities right now? What "categories" in your life are you prioritizing? Your health? Wealth? Marriage? A specific skillset or project or initiative?

Before you proceed to the next step, pinpoint your top *five* strategic priorities, or goals below. The hard work here has already been done back in Chapter 4. If need be, revisit that earlier list of fifty goals to guide you.

1. _____

2. _____

3. _____

4. _____

5. _____

Step 2: Find your 5.

The 80/20 rule, a.k.a., the Pareto Principle, states that 80 percent of your actions produce just 20 percent of your results. The uncomfortable truth is that most of us

Do you think Richard Branson got rich and then got clear on his priorities . . . or do you think he got clear on his priorities and then got rich?

spend our lives doing the 80 percent of things that produce only 20 percent of our results.

The trivial tasks. The time-wasting busy work. The things that never move the needle. Even when we're focused, we're often focused on the wrong things or actions. That's why 80 percent of what you're doing right now could be meaningless.

But the Pareto Principle states the opposite is also true. Just 20 percent of your actions produce 80 percent of your results.

Wouldn't you like to do more of the 20 and less of the 80? The goal seems so simple: Do more of the things that produce results and fewer of the things that don't. Or do less to accomplish more.

But what if we take it a step further? What if we *really* magnify your focus? As you can see below, if 20 percent of your actions produce 80 percent of your results, then 5 percent of your actions could produce 95 percent of your results.

Want to magnify your focus? Want to skyrocket your value? Want to separate yourself? Find your "5 percent," and focus on that.

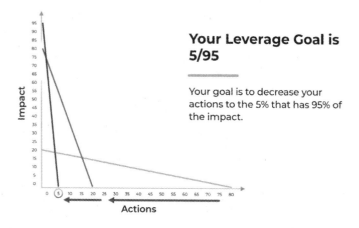

Your Leverage Goal is 5/95

Your goal is to decrease your actions to the 5% that has 95% of the impact.

But here's another way to look at that 5 percent. Think of this as five *actions* that will produce 95 percent of your results as you strive to achieve your strategic priorities. Your five "high-impact actions," or what I call your HIAs. You see, magnifying your focus isn't about doing 15, 50, or 105 things. Remember, multitasking is a lie. It's about finding your five high-impact actions for each of your strategic priorities and focusing on them.

For example, John Maxwell's number one strategic priority is to write books. So he does five things every single day, his five high-impact actions: read, think, file, ask questions, and write. As you can see, his actions are simple, not complex. And every day means every day. The simplicity is critical, and the consistency is key. By focusing on his five high-impact actions every day, John's written more than one hundred books. In other words, he's crushed his top strategic priority by focusing on five simple things.

What are your five high-impact actions?

Pick your top strategic priority, then find your five below. In other words, pinpoint the five high-impact actions only you can do to accomplish that priority. Then magnify your focus on those five things by doing them every day. I encourage you to do this same exercise for each of your other four strategic priorities as well. Find your five, focus on your five, and you'll be amazed at how much more you can accomplish by getting focused and doing less.

1. _____

2. _____

3. _____

4. _____

5. _____

Step 3: Throw away the rest.

You know what you want to accomplish—your strategic priorities. And you know what you need to do—your five high-impact actions for each. But now, let me ask you, "What do you need to *stop* doing?"

What you *don't* do is just as important as what you choose to do.

What do you need to remove from your routine? What do you need to add to what Warren Buffett calls your "avoid-at-all-cost list" or your "not-to-do list"? Maybe you need to turn off those pesky cell phone notifications so you can create instead of consume. Maybe you need to unplug the television so you can read instead of react. Maybe you need to cancel happy hour so you can schedule time for skill development. Maybe you need to audit your inner circle, or your "33," and avoid specific people so you listen to others who say you can.

When it comes to focus, what you *don't* do is just as important as what you choose to do. Richard Branson said "No" to say "Yes." Said differently, he says "no" to low-impact actions. What do you need to say no to so you can say yes to your strategic priorities and high-impact actions?

Throw away the trivial many. They are nothing more than distractions. Focus on the critical few. You can think of this as addition by subtraction.

Pinpoint your top five strategic priorities. Find your five high-impact actions for each. And throw your low-impact actions on your avoid-at-all-costs list. Snap out of "the Matrix" and harness your superpower.

"Be the one" who magnifies their focus.

CHAPTER
11

Be Urgent

How much urgency do you have in your life right now? Do you chase your dreams with urgency? Do you tackle your goals with urgency? Do you treat every day with urgency? Or do you need to start living your life and writing your story with more pace, pep, and urgency?

What's your relationship with death? What if death is *life's* greatest driving force? What if death can become *your* greatest driving force?

You see, Steve Jobs implored us to use our own death as a tool. "Death is very likely the single best invention of life," he said. Jobs shared that sentiment with a group of early twenty somethings, nonetheless, during his 2005 Stanford commencement speech. Think about that. One of the most illustrious inventors, or creators, of our lifetime referred to death as the "single best invention of life."

How would you live if you knew you were dying? What would you do? What would you say? What would you think? What wouldn't you do, say, or think? Is there a reason you're not living like that right now?

You and I were born with a death sentence. None of us are getting out of this thing alive. It's a fact that we all inch closer to death every day. And I don't say that to be morbid. I say it to be motivating. The great Roman emperor Marcus Aurelius said, "*Memento mori*," which means "meditate on mortality."

What if death is life's greatest driving force? What if mortality is life's greatest motivator? Why don't we use our mortality as a "tool" to chisel an extraordinary life?

"You could leave life right now," Aurelius added in his timeless series of personal essays, titled *Meditations*. "Let that determine what you do and say and think."

Our lives are limited because our time is limited. Yet so many of us live as if we have all the time in the world. We waste it. We burn it. We take it for granted. We live casually.

How many times have you pushed something off until tomorrow? How many times will you wait until you're "ready"? When *will* you be ready? If not now, when? How many times have you postponed the trip,

What if death is life's greatest driving force? What if mortality is life's greatest motivator?

the date night, or the event? How often do you catch yourself procrastinating? How often do you wait?

These are telltale signs of a casual life. And a casual life is not an intentional life.

Did you know the average American dies at approximately seventy-nine years old? Seventy-nine might seem like lifetimes away, but think about this: at just forty years old, your life could already be half over. My life is already half over. That motivates me. The way I see it, I've got less time to do more.

Plus, we sleep through a full third of our life. For most of us, about eight of our twenty-four hours each day are spent sleeping. And another third of our hours, and years, are filled with things like school, eating, messing around on our phones, and ironically, trying to fall asleep.

This means that 66 percent of your time is already accounted for, which leaves 33 percent, or one-third, for so-called "free" time. But we've already established that your time isn't really free; it has value. Lots of it.

Steve Jobs died at just fifty-six years old. Marcus Aurelius died at fifty-eight. Yet, look at how much both men accomplished.

The reality is, you can't buy back time. You can't add years to your life. But you can add life to your years. To do that, though, you have to stop living casually.

In 1787, James Madison, John Jay, and Alexander Hamilton, three of America's founding fathers, began penning a series of essays that became known as *The Federalist Papers*. These pieces were written to influence voters to ratify, or accept, the new US constitution. The plan was to write a total of twenty-five essays to persuade the public. The work was distributed among the three men; John Jay wrote five, James Madison wrote twenty-nine, and Alexander Hamilton wrote the other fifty-one. They wrote eighty-five essays in total—in just six months. The last of the essays was published in May 1788, and the constitution was ratified the following month. And the process of organizing the new government began soon after.

Historian Garry Wills observed that what made *The Federalist Papers* so effective and influential was the rapid pace at which they were written. As Wills put it, the speed at which they were written and released "overwhelmed" any possible response.

(That's an interesting word, *pace*. Are you living with a certain pace? Or are you living casually?)

In fact, these events are depicted in the musical *Hamilton*, and the song "Non-Stop" is an entire ode to Alexander Hamilton's urgency. Throughout the song, Hamilton asks one question repeatedly, "Why do you write like you're running out of time? Write day and night like you're running out of time."

Do you know why Alexander Hamilton wrote like he was "running out of time?" Because he was! He was killed in a duel by the third vice president of the United States, Aaron Burr, and died at age forty-seven. He was running out of time. And, my friend, so are you!

Get some mortality motivation. Write your life story with urgency. Live with urgency.

Hamilton wasn't frantic. He was focused; he had focused urgency. Steve Jobs had focused urgency, and Marcus Aurelius had focused urgency. Are you living with focused urgency?

Social psychologists say that, at the end of our lives, 84 percent of our regret is not for things that we did wrong, or the mistakes we made, but for all the things we didn't do.[28] In other words, our biggest regrets are created by inaction. The goals we didn't chase. The courage we didn't have. The dreams we didn't pursue. The risks we didn't take. We regret most the things that were casualties of our casualness, probably because we thought we had time. Unfortunately, the bill for regret far outweighs the cost of urgency.

Ask Jobs. Ask Aurelius. Ask Hamilton. Life goes fast.

Don't put off what can be done today until tomorrow. Live with focused urgency.

Let me share a quote that gives me chills to this day. LA Lakers legend Kobe Bryant once said, "The biggest mistake we make in life is believing we have time." Bryant died at just forty-one years old, but look at what he accomplished. Heck, he didn't just live with focused

In other words, our biggest regrets are created by inaction. The goals we didn't chase. The courage we didn't have. The dreams we didn't pursue. The risks we didn't take.

urgency, he pushed his young teammates to live with focused urgency too. He said, "If you're patiently going about it, you'll never get there." In other words: We need to get better. *You* need to get better. Now.

Don't live casually any longer. Don't wait for tomorrow. Don't take your time here for granted. Time's running out with your parents. Time's running out with your kids. Time's running out, period.

Write your life story like you're running out of time.

Remember you could leave life right now. From this moment on, let that determine what you do, say, and think. Don't wait for things to change. Don't wait until it's convenient. Don't wait until you're motivated. Don't wait until you're ready. Don't wait until tomorrow.

What dream do you need to chase right now? What family member do you need to call right now? What goal do you need to work toward right now? What action do you need to take right now? What do you need to finally stop waiting on?

Commit yourself to living with urgency, *focused* urgency, here and now. From this day forward, commit to doing everything with pace. Commit to living with "mortality motivation." Commit to living like you're running out of time. Commit to accomplishing more in less time. Commit to valuing every minute you have left. Commit to getting more urgent, being more urgent, now.

"Be the one" who lives with urgency.

Be Unforgettable

As I mentioned earlier, I've had the privilege of participating in several "country transformations" with John C. Maxwell and a small group of his closest confidants. My son Isaac joined us for one of our country transformations in Costa Rica.

At the time, Isaac was just seventeen years old, the youngest person in the group by decades, a teenager surrounded by accomplished consultants, executives, and business leaders, sharing rooms with heads of state, leaders in sports, and local icons.

On our first night in Costa Rica, we shared a small, intimate steak dinner as a group. We were seated on the dimly lit patio of the hotel restaurant and surrounded by swaying palms. It was me, Isaac, John, and nine others, including Mark Cole (CEO of Maxwell Organization) and Jeff Stewart (founder of Keller Williams Asheville), encircling a round table reserved for our group. While I was catching up with Mark, Jeff, and the rest of the group, I spotted Isaac and John having what appeared to be a deep and meaningful conversation.

I've always admired how John includes my son. John was the most accomplished person at that table—and typically the most accomplished person at any table at any steakhouse in any country—yet he had no problem giving Isaac, a high school kid, his undivided attention.

After dinner, Isaac and I stepped into an empty elevator together. As the doors slid closed, Isaac turned to me and asked the most genuine question, "Dad . . . how can I add value to John Maxwell?" He recognized that he had gotten a lot from John—as this dinner wasn't their first conversation. And he wanted to give back.

Candidly, I remember thinking to myself: *Son, you can't. You're a teenager, a kid. John's a living legend. He doesn't need, nor does he want, anything from you. I love and admire how much you care. But just enjoy the trip.*

Of course, I didn't say a word of that. The last thing I wanted to do was dismiss my son. I could see the sincerity in his eyes. I could hear the passion in his voice. I could almost feel how much this meant to him. So rather than haphazardly blurt out the first thing that came to mind, I suggested we take some time to think. I said to Isaac, "Let's brainstorm."

As we thought through how Isaac could add value to John's life, an idea hit me.

"Hey Isaac . . ."

"Yeah?"

"What if you wrote John a note? Like a hand-written note . . ."

I figured in today's digital world, anything hand-written shows an uncommon level of effort and care. It's rare. And the rarer something is, the more value it has. Be it a painting, a diamond, or even a friendship, anything that is rare is more valuable. That's why I was confident a hand-written note could "add value" to John.

Isaac quietly took the idea in. I could almost see the wheels turning in his head. Does a note add enough value? Is it a big enough deal? Do I even have something to share that will be meaningful to John?

The answer was yes.

For the remainder of the trip, I'd catch glimpses of Isaac deep in thought, gazing down at the lined pages of a notebook, his forehead resting on one hand, the other gripping a pen that would periodically flow across the page. A visible sign of the tremendous thought Isaac poured into that note was that he took his time writing it. He spent days on it, injecting the perfect word or phrase here and there, adding a single sentence or two,

And the rarer
something is, the
more value it has.
Be it a painting,
a diamond, or
even a friendship,
anything that
is rare is more
valuable.

at what seemed like each stop we made. Our hotel room. Restaurants. Conference rooms. You name it.

He used his phone as a research tool to create, not consume. He was focused, maybe even fixated, on his mission to add value. He didn't just whip up a short, expected thank-you note to John. He ended up writing him a full-blown letter, filling an entire 8.5 x 11 sheet of loose-leaf. And to my surprise, he didn't write just one letter. He wrote ten. He penned a hand-written letter for each of the nine *other* individuals on the trip.

Jeff Stewart pulled me aside after reading Isaac's letter to him. And I'll never forget what he said because it nearly brought me to tears.

"Justin . . . I have two young sons. If my sons ever write a letter like the one your son just wrote to me, it will be my proudest day as a father."

As our trip came to an end, John had one final speech left to give. He asked us to join him in the green room beforehand. Picture all twelve of us seated in a circle. John, Mark, Jeff, Isaac, me, and the rest of the group. We were like a sports team, huddled up together for a final moment with our leader, John.

"As you leave this trip," he said, "I have one last piece of advice for you . . . be unforgettable."

"How can you be more unforgettable?" he continued, pausing between each question to let his words sink in. "How can you be more unforgettable in your conversations? How can you be more unforgettable to your clients? To your friends? To your family? To your colleagues? To your kids? To the people who need you? To the people who listen to you?"

John treated each question like a calling, one inviting us to uncover the answers in our heads. Then he challenged us with a final, all-encompassing question: "How can you live an unforgettable life?"

You could hear, see, and feel his conviction every time he repeated that word, *unforgettable*. It was no different than the conviction radiating from Isaac when he asked me how he could add value to John in the hotel elevator just a few days earlier. Then just when we thought John was done speaking, he peeled open the flap of his jet-black suit coat and dug into the interior pocket. He gently removed a folded piece of paper and carefully unfolded it out in front of him for all of us to see. An 8.5 x 11 sheet of loose-leaf.

Then he turned to my son. "Isaac," he said. "You are unforgettable. This letter is unforgettable."

Think about that. This was a small group of highly successful and respected men and women. People who had spent decades making an impact. Yet the youngest one in the room was the most unforgettable person there. Because he asked—and answered—one simple question.

His question revealed a secret to being unforgettable, maybe *the* secret to being unforgettable. And it's the same question I challenge you to ask yourself: How do I add value? How do I add value to my clients? To my friends? To my family? To my colleagues? To my kids? To the people who need me? To the people who listen to me?

That's how the trip ended. But that's not the end of this story.

When we got back home to St. George, Utah, Isaac received a package in the mail. A brown box that contained a beautiful Montblanc pen engraved with his initials on it, along with a hand-written letter. A letter from the man who sent it: Jeff Stewart.

His question revealed a secret to being unforgettable, maybe *the* secret to being unforgettable. And it's the same question I challenge you to ask yourself: How do I add value?

Jeff wrote to Isaac to share some news about his office in Asheville. His Keller Williams headquarters. There was something new hanging on the wall.

Any guesses?

Turns out, it was Isaac's letter to Jeff, the one hand-written and hand-delivered in Costa Rica. It was now framed and displayed publicly for everybody who entered the office to see, setting the tone for headquarters, to encourage everyone to, you guessed it, add value. And therefore, to be unforgettable.

My friend, all of this happened by answering one simple question: How can I add value?

As we conclude this chapter, ask yourself that same question. *How can I add value?* Don't haphazardly fill this page. Remember, service to many leads to greatness. Be thoughtful. Be intentional. Be bold. Be specific. Be vivid. Pen your answers in the space below to transport them from your head to your heart. Declare them on these pages. Then, as Isaac did, take action. "Be the one" who adds value.

"Be the one" who is unforgettable.

_____

_____

_____

_____

13

"Be the One" Who Wins Both Races

I'd like to end our journey together by sharing two things with you. My philosophy on life, *and* what I believe about you.

Let's start with my philosophy on life. I believe life is made up of two races, two that we all should be running. And just like any other race, there are winners and losers. Which raises questions I often ask myself before starting any endeavor: What does winning look like? And what are the rules? In other words, how do I win?

The first race is the one you're probably familiar with. The race for success. Winning at this is measured by things like money, property, accolades, recognition, influence, fame, fortune, etc. The kinds of things that scream "success" to the average person.

It's the race pretty much everyone's running. And it's the race pretty much everyone's trying to win. But it's not the *only* race.

Let me tell you about the second one. It's the race for a superior form of success. A race worth more than money. It's the race for all the things that really matter in your life. Your faith, your relationship with your family, your relationship with others. It's the way you serve and show up. It's the impact you have. And it's the mark you make.

The second race is the race for your legacy.

So I think of it like this: life's first race is material; the second race is generational.

I see so many people running the first race but losing the second. They sacrifice their legacy for greed. Their family for fame. Their morals for followers.

But what happens if you win the first race and lose the second?

You still lose.

What's the point of being rich if you're miserable? Like religious leader and educator David O. McKay would say, "No other success can compensate for failure in the home." Winning the first race isn't worth losing the second race.

But here's what's really interesting: The opposite is also true. Like I said, many people run the first race and

Life's first race is material; the second race is generational.

lose the second. But I also see people running the second race *while* losing the first. Some of them don't even enter the first race. They never step over the start line or push off from the starting blocks. They think money is the root of all evil. They feel they have to be poor to be righteous. But you don't have to avoid the material to maintain your morals. You don't have to pawn your valuables for your values.

Again, if you ask me, that's not winning. That's losing. These people play small. They conceal their dreams. They bury their talents. They hide their gifts. They don't turn into the person they were born to become. And the truth is, you can do more good when you have more resources to do good with.

The bottom line is, you can run both races. And you can *win* both races. In other words, I believe you can have it all.

You can do good and do well at the same time. You can be rich and righteous. You can love your life and leave a legacy. And I'm rooting for you to win both of life's races.

But guess what?

I'm not the only one rooting for you. As I mentioned before, the "ancestral math" shows you have 4,094 ancestors rooting for you too. That's twelve generations of your flesh and blood cheering you on. They may be gone, but I believe their legacy and their souls live on.

You can do good and do well at the same time. You can be rich and righteous. You can love your life and leave a legacy.

Your grandma. Your grandpa. Your great-grandma. Your great-grandpa. Your ancestors who already ran life's races. They're cheering for you from the sidelines.

Imagine that.

Think about them. Run for them. Win for them. That's what "the one" does.

Looking back to what I shared at the beginning of our journey together, on that Memorial Day morning at the cemetery with my son, I could feel my fifth-generation grandpa George Prince's presence. I know that may sound sensationalized, but it's the truth. He was there with me. He was there with Isaac. He was there to cheer us on. He was telling me I have what it takes to "be the one." He was telling my son the same.

George is just one of 4,094 souls I run both races for.

Who are you running life's races for?

Don't just look back. Look forward too. What about your family members who are running now? Your siblings. Your kids. Your nieces. Your nephews.

What about your descendants, patiently waiting for their turn to run, to launch off the starting blocks? Your kids' kids. Their kids' kids. Your fifth- and sixth-generation grandchildren and beyond.

Your ancestors are cheering for you. Your descendants are counting on you. They all want you to win both races. They need you to win both races.

My kids are counting on me as I counted on George.

Who's counting on you? Who's cheering you on? Run for them. Win for them.

That's what "the one" does.

You now know the rules of life's two races. They've been revealed to you in this book, one by one, chapter by chapter, which means you now know how to win both races.

Simply follow the rules . . .

Create and design your future.

Live an intentional life.

Update your identity.

Clarify your "3D" vision.

Build your 3 Cs—confidence, commitment, and competence.

Elevate your emotional maturity.

Amplify your associations.

Speak life into your future.

Stack reasons to keep going.

Magnify your focus.

Be urgent.

Be unforgettable.

Be the one.

Go to IamJustinPrince.com/BetheOne to unlock additional tools, resources, and wisdom to help you be "the one."

ACKNOWLEDGMENTS

I owe a debt of gratitude to the many people who have made this book a reality, and I would like to take a moment to thank several of them.

First and foremost, my heartfelt thanks goes out to my incredible wife and constant support, Missy. Thank you for being my rock. You are the best decision I have ever made, and without you, I wouldn't "be the one" to write this book. I love you, sweetheart. And I am forever grateful for your love, support, and all that you do.

To my amazing kids—Isaac, Ciera, Lexi, and AJ—you are the light of my life. My desire to make you proud has been the catalyst for all the good that has happened in my life. Each of you is an incredible person—unique, talented, and inspiring—and a shining example of "the one." You are all leaders in your own right, and I am in awe of the positive impact you have on my world—and *the* world. I am so proud to be your dad, and I love you more than anything.

I am immensely grateful for my coauthor, Clay Manley, who helped me to organize my thoughts and my message, propel this project forward, and translate my heart, experiences, and principles into the words that fill this book. Clay, your passion for life, relentless attention to detail, and unwillingness to cut corners were instrumental. Writing is your gift, and I am honored and grateful that you shared it with me and our readers.

My heartfelt gratitude goes out to my amazing teams, both internal and external, who have been an integral part of my journey. To Amanda, Katie, Ty, and the rest of my internal team, thank you for your unwavering support, dedication, and hard work. To everyone at Modere, thank you for your incredible talent, passion, and commitment to excellence. I am a better person for knowing all of you, and I am forever grateful to do life and business with such incredible individuals.

To my dear parents, brothers, and sisters, whose unwavering love and support have been the bedrock upon which my life was built. You helped mold me in those early years, and your encouragement and support have been a source of strength and inspiration throughout my journey. I am forever grateful for each of you, and I thank you from the bottom of my heart.

And to the publishing team at Forefront Books and the Maxwell Leadership Publishing Family—Justin, Jen, Jill, and others—thank you for helping to get this over the finish line and into the hands and hearts of "the one."

ENDNOTES

1. Benjamin Franklin, *Poor Richard's Almanack,* 1733.
2. Lewis Howes, "Les Brown: Overcome All Odds and Change the World," November 7, 2017, in *The School of Greatness,* podcast, https://lewishowes.com/podcast/i-les-brown-overcome-all-odds-and-change-the-world/.
3. "The Story You Believe About Yourself Determines Success," keynote speech by Les Brown, SUCCESS Live, September 8, 2017, video, https://www.youtube.com/watch?v=68Wz25NMX2k.
4. William W. George and Andrew N. McLean, *Anne Mulcahy: Leading Xerox through the Perfect Storm,* case 405-050, (Boston, MA: Harvard Business School, 2005).
5. Staff, "The Cow in the Ditch: How Anne Mulcahy Rescued Xerox," *Knowledge at Wharton,* (November 2005), https://knowledge.wharton.upenn.edu/article/the-cow-in-the-ditch-how-anne-mulcahy-rescued-xerox/.
6. Lisa Vollmer, "Anne Mulcahy: The Keys to Turnaround at Xerox," *Stanford Business,* December 01, 2004, https://www.gsb.stanford.edu/insights/anne-mulcahy-keys-turnaround-xerox.

7. Anne M. Mulcahy, "American Innovation: A competitive Crisis" (speech, The Chief Executives' Club of Boston, Boston, MA, June 12, 2008).

8. "Anne M. Mulcahy," Inductees, Connecticut Women's Hall of Fame, 2010, https://www.cwhf.org/inductees/anne -m-mulcahy.

9. Anne Mulcahy, "View from the Top Speaker Series," December 2004, Stanford Graduate School of Business, Stanford University, video recording, https://www.youtube .com/watch?v=Q_hRTyllwC4.

10. Betsy Morris, "The Accidental CEO: She Was Never Groomed to Be the Boss, But Anne Mulcahy is Bring- ing Xerox Back From the Dead," *CNN Money*, June 23, 2003, https://money.cnn.com/magazines/fortune/fortune _archive/2003/06/23/344603/index.htm.

11. Jacquie McNish, "Xerox's Success is a Reflection of Her Dedication," *The Globe and Mail*, September 11, 2008, https://www.theglobeandmail.com/report-on-business /xeroxs-success-is-a-reflection-of-her-dedication/article 715942/.

12. Marcel Schwantes, "Science Says 92 Percent of Peo- ple Don't Achieve Their Goals. Here's How the Other 8 Percent Do," *Inc.* July 26, 2016, https://www.inc.com /marcel-schwantes/science-says-92-percent-of-people-dont -achieve-goals-heres-how-the-other-8-perce.html.

13. Og Mandino, *The Greatest Secret in the World*, rev. ed. (North Bay Village, FL: Frederick Fell Publishers, 2009).

14. Matt Barnes and Stephen Jackson, "Kenny Smith," June 2, 2022, in *All the Smoke*, podcast, https://www.youtube.com /watch?v=IkIpCBUgcWQ.

15. Nicholas A Christakis and James H. Fowler, "The Spread of Obesity in a Large Social Network over 32 Years," *The New*

England Journal of Medicine, 357, no. 4 (July 2007): 370-79, https://www.nejm.org/doi/full/10.1056/nejmsa066082.

16. Inga Kiderra, "Obesity Is 'Socially Contagious,' Study Finds," *University Communications & Public Relations Materials: News Releases,* July 25, 2007, https://library.ucsd.edu/dc/object/bb93927660.

17. Gina Kolata, "Study Says Obesity Can be Contagious," *The New York Times,* July 25, 2007, https://www.nytimes.com/2007/07/25/health/25cnd-fat.html.

18. Tom Bilyeu, "Trevor Moawad: Mindset Expert Shows You How to Control Your Negative Thoughts," March 3, 2020 in *Impact Theory,* web series, https://impacttheory.com/episode/trevor-moawad/.

19. Alexander Ritter, Marcel Franz, Wolfgang H. R. Miltner, Thomas Weis, "How Words Impact on Pain," *Brain and Behavior,* 9, no. 9 (August 2019): https://pubmed.ncbi.nlm.nih.gov/31368674/.

20. Edward Luker, "Are Video Games, Screens Another Addiction?" *Speaking of Health, Mayo Clinic Health System,* July 1, 2022, https://www.mayoclinichealthsystem.org/hometown-health/speaking-of-health/are-video-games-and-screens-another-addiction.

21. Alex Kerai, "2023 Cell Phone Usage Statistics: Mornings Are for Notifications," *reviews.org,* May 9, 2023, https://www.reviews.org/mobile/cell-phone-addiction/.

22. Travis Bradberry, "Multitasking Damages Your Brain and Career, New Studies Suggest," *Forbes,* October 8, 2014, https://www.forbes.com/sites/travisbradberry/2014/10/08/multitasking-damages-your-brain-and-career-new-studies-suggest/?sh=961a91c56ee6.

23. Roman Povolotskiy, Nakul Gupta, Adam B. Leverant, "Head and Neck Injuries Associated with Cell Phone Use,"

JAMA Otolaryngology Head and Neck Surgery, 146, no. 2, (December 2019): https://jamanetwork.com/journals /jamaotolaryngology/fullarticle/2756314.

24. Sandee LaMotte, "Walking While Texting and Other Cell Phone Related Injuries Are on the Rise, Especially for the Young," *CNN Health*, December 5, 2019, https://www .cnn.com/2019/12/05/health/cell-phone-injury-increase -texting-wellness/index.html#:~:text=A%20new%20study %20analyzing%20national,texting%20with%20a%20cell %20phone.

25. Jackie Salo, "The Average Person Spends 78K Hours of Their Lives Watching TV: Study," *New York Post*, December 3, 2019, https://nypost.com/2019/12/03/the-average-person -spends-78k-hours-of-their-lives-watching-tv-study/#.

26. Andrea Herron, "Want to Be More Productive? You Might Need to Put Your Phone in Another Room," *WebMD*, December 10, 2019, https://www.webmdhealthservices .com/blog/want-to-be-more-productive-you-might -need-to-put-your-phone-in-another-room/#:~:text=You %20Might%20Need%20to%20Put%20Your%20Phone %20in%20Another%20Room,-Andrea%20Herron&text =Between%20push%20notifications%2C%20texts%2C %20meeting,on%20our%20ability%20to%20focus.

27. Peter Suciu, "American Spent On Average More Than 1,300 Hours on Social media Last Year," *Forbes*, June 24, 2021, https://www.forbes.com/sites/petersuciu/2021/06/24 /americans-spent-more-than-1300-hours-on-social-media /?sh=f02866c2547f.

28. Thomas Glovich and Victoria Husted Medvec, "The Experience of Regret: What, When, and Why," *Psychological Review, American Psychological Association*, 102, no. 2 (April 1995): https://psycnet.apa.org/doiLanding?doi=10 .1037%2F0033-295X.102.2.379